# THE SIMPLE TIME MANAGEMENT GUIDE FOR PROFESSIONALS

PROVEN STRATEGIES TO HELP YOU SUCCEED, FOCUS, BOOST EFFICIENCY, BALANCE LIFE, ACCELERATE YOUR CAREER & GIVE YOU THE FREEDOM TO ENJOY LIFE

FREEDOM PUBLICATIONS

**Copyright © 2025 Freedom Publications. All rights reserved.**

The content within this book may not be reproduced, duplicated, or transmitted without direct written permission from the author or the publisher.

Under no circumstances will any blame or legal responsibility be held against the publisher, or author, for any damages, reparation, or monetary loss due to the information contained within this book, either directly or indirectly.

**Legal Notice:**

This book is copyright protected. It is only for personal use. You cannot amend, distribute, sell, use, quote, or paraphrase any part of the content within this book, without the consent of the author or publisher.

**Disclaimer Notice:**

Please note the information contained within this document is for educational and entertainment purposes only. All effort has been expended to present accurate, up-to-date, reliable, and complete information. No warranties of any kind are declared or implied. Readers acknowledge that the author is not engaged in the rendering of legal, financial, medical, or professional advice. The content within this book has been derived from various sources. Please consult a licensed professional before attempting any techniques outlined in this book.

By reading this document, the reader agrees that under no circumstances is the author responsible for any losses, direct or indirect, that are incurred as a result of the use of the information contained within this document, including, but not limited to, errors, omissions, or inaccuracies.

# CONTENTS

| | |
|---|---|
| *Introduction* | 5 |
| 1. Building a Strong Foundation for Time Mastery | 11 |
| 2. Mastering Your Mind Set | 35 |
| 3. Balancing Work and Personal Life | 47 |
| 4. Sustaining and Adapting Your Time Management Strategies | 67 |
| 5. Mastering the Art of Delegation for Better Time Management | 85 |
| *Conclusion* | 97 |
| *Glossary of Terms* | 105 |
| *References* | 109 |
| *About the Publisher* | 111 |

# INTRODUCTION
## TAKING CONTROL OF YOUR TIME

In today's fast-paced world, time has become more elusive than ever. As demands continue to mount, many professionals know all too well the feeling of trying to fit an impossible to-do list into a day that ends before we feel ready. Hours seem to vanish, often without a true sense of accomplishment. Studies show that nearly half of people feel they lack the time to fulfil their daily demands. This is especially challenging for professionals who are learning to balance multiple responsibilities; work, family, and personal growth, often for the first time. It can feel as though time itself is slipping away, reminding us just how essential effective time management has become. Today, time management is not just a helpful tool or a nice-to-have skill; it is an absolute necessity for anyone looking to lead a balanced, fulfilling life.

This book exists to help you take on this universal challenge and reshape the way you approach time management. Managing time well isn't only about fitting more into each day; it's about regaining control, clarity, and a sense of purpose in how you use your hours. The techniques outlined in these pages are designed to do just that, providing practical, actionable strategies that allow you to quickly take back control over your schedule and destiny. Best of all, these strategies are realistic and accessible. You won't need to master complex planning systems or follow rigid routines to see results. Instead, this book offers solutions that professionals can use to see real improvements in their lives right away.

At Freedom Publications, our passion lies in helping professionals like you tackle the challenges of time management. We have seen first-hand how simple, practical changes can transform not just the flow of a day but the quality of life as a whole. Over the years, we have guided clients from feeling overwhelmed and constantly behind to experiencing balance, productivity, and a renewed sense of calm. This transformation is possible and sustainable, and our aim in writing this book is to share that journey with you. The techniques you will discover here are not just theories but strategies that are tried, tested and refined to ensure they are both effective and easy to apply.

One of the biggest reasons many professionals struggle with time management is *procrastination*. We have all felt that urge to delay a task, rationalising that "I'll be more motivated later" or "I work better under pressure." But too often, procrastination leads to unnecessary stress and a rushed or lower-quality outcome. Procrastination, however, isn't the only hurdle; *prioritisation* can be just as challenging. With so many competing demands, it can feel difficult to decide what to tackle first; emails, projects, personal commitments. Without a clear plan, it's easy to fall into the trap of task-switching, which usually leads to a lack of progress in any one area. There's also the issue of *work-life balance*, as work tasks spill into personal time, draining energy and leaving little room for relationships or self-care. Yet, even with these common obstacles, there is a path forward.

By committing to the techniques in this book, you'll gain the tools to master time management, transforming your days from chaos to calm and fulfilment. Imagine a life where you end each day with satisfaction, no longer feeling defeated by what's left undone. Picture a rhythm that allows you to meet your professional responsibilities while still making time for yourself and the people who matter most.

This book is designed to take you on a path of growth, giving you the tools to redefine your relationship with time. Each chapter focuses on a core theme, from foundational concepts like identifying your unique time management challenges to practical tools for handling procrastination, breaking down large tasks, and creating routines that foster focus. We'll begin by identifying your personal obstacles and the underlying psychology behind habits like procrastination. Then, we'll move into practical techniques, such as breaking tasks into manageable parts, minimising distractions, and building routines that promote productivity.

The focus here isn't just on understanding these techniques but on applying them to real life. You'll find examples to illustrate each strategy, along with exercises to help you implement these ideas immediately. For example, when we discuss prioritisation, you'll learn approaches like the ABCDE method and the MoSCoW framework. These techniques will help you prioritise tasks and provide clarity as you move through your day with purpose. When we address procrastination, you'll discover tools like the Pomodoro Technique, which uses timed work sessions to build momentum, and task segmentation, which makes larger tasks feel more manageable.

As you progress through this journey, we encourage you to actively engage. Reflect on what you have learned, consider your habits, experiment with techniques, and observe what resonates.

Effective time management isn't one-size-fits-all, so exploring these strategies with an open mind will help you discover which methods best support your unique lifestyle, goals, and challenges. *Consider keeping a journal* as you read, tracking your progress, noting insights, and recording any changes in your routine. This journal will not only help maintain motivation but also allow you to witness how far you've come.

Ultimately, time management is about more than fitting tasks into a day; it's about aligning your time with your values and priorities. Mastering your time gives you the freedom to focus on what truly matters to you. Whether that's being more present with family, returning to a beloved hobby, or pursuing a major career goal. Effective time management empowers you to create a life that reflects those values.

At its core, this book is a call to action. It's an invitation to take control of your time, transform your habits, and improve your quality of life. If you're ready to begin this journey, put in the effort, and explore new ways of managing your day, then this book will be an invaluable companion. Each chapter is filled with strategies to help you build a solid foundation in time management, from setting goals and overcoming procrastination to creating efficient routines and protecting your work-life balance.

View this journey as an investment in yourself. Time is finite; once it's gone, you cannot get it back. By dedicating yourself to mastering these skills, you're giving yourself the gift of a more organised, fulfilling life. Imagine the peace that comes from knowing you're in control of your schedule, with time for what matters most and freedom from the tyranny of the endless to-do list. This is your guide to reclaiming control, building routines that serve your goals, and experiencing the profound transformation that effective time management can bring. Together, let's take that first step toward a more productive, balanced, and fulfilling life.

# 1

# BUILDING A STRONG FOUNDATION FOR TIME MASTERY

In this first chapter, we will lay the groundwork for your journey toward mastering time management. By the chapter's end, you'll have built a personalised foundation designed to support your goals and daily demands, and you'll be better equipped to manage your time, boost productivity, and improve your work-life balance. This chapter focuses on understanding the root of common time management challenges, clarifying your goals, and establishing systems for accountability and reflection. With these essential building blocks, you'll be ready to take control of your time and productivity in a way that works for you and allows for sustainable improvement over time.

In today's busy world, balancing personal and professional demands can be difficult, with tasks and responsibilities often seeming endless. If you've ever felt like you were struggling to keep up or unable to finish the projects you care about most, know that you're not alone. Many professionals face similar challenges.

In this chapter, we will address the fundamental issues that disrupt effective time management, including overloaded task lists, constant digital distractions, difficulty prioritising, and the cycle of procrastination. We'll also introduce actionable methods to overcome these obstacles.

Let's dive into each of these building blocks to start creating a more balanced, focused, and productive approach to your work and life.

## PINPOINTING YOUR PERSONAL TIME MANAGEMENT CHALLENGES

For many, time management issues are rooted in several common obstacles. Recognising these obstacles is crucial, as they are often the unseen forces that derail plans, disrupt productivity, and drain energy. Below, we'll explore each of these common pitfalls and provide targeted strategies for addressing them.

1. **The Overwhelming Task List**

One of the most daunting challenges in time management is the never-ending to-do list. When the list seems too long to tackle, it's easy to feel overwhelmed, often leading to a "paralysis by analysis" effect that can make it difficult to get started on anything. Many people respond to this feeling of overwhelm by procrastinating, and delaying tasks until they feel even more pressed for time. This often leads to a stressful cycle of low productivity and potential burnout.

To combat this, *start by categorising tasks based on importance and urgency.* Write down everything on your to-do list, and use a prioritisation tool like the ***Eisenhower Matrix*** to classify each item into four categories:

- **Urgent and Important:** Tackle these tasks immediately, as they have the highest impact and can be critical for success.
- **Not Urgent but Important:** Schedule these tasks for later but keep them visible to ensure they're not forgotten. They may be long-term goals and tasks that require planning and focus.
- **Urgent but Not Important:** Delegate these tasks to others whenever possible to free up your time.
- **Not Urgent and Not Important:** Consider removing or rescheduling these to focus on higher-priority tasks, as these can be distractions or low-value activities, so avoid or eliminate them.

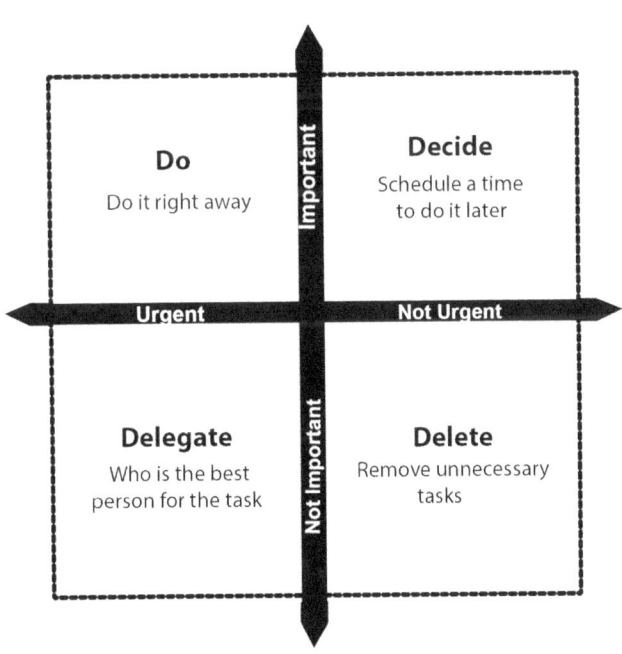

The Eisenhower Matrix

Breaking down your tasks into manageable categories and setting clear priorities helps prevent overwhelm and enables you to approach each day with a clear direction.

### 2. The Digital Distraction Trap

Today there is so much technology, making distractions almost impossible to avoid. Social media, emails, and constant notifications pull us away from focused work, making it difficult to stay on track. Studies reveal that every time we lose focus, it takes about 25 minutes to fully regain our previous level of concentration. This digital distraction loop can hinder productivity, making deep work nearly impossible and leaving us feeling scattered.

To avoid this, you can *create dedicated "no distraction" blocks* throughout your day to focus on high-priority tasks without interruptions. During these blocks, consider using tools like *Focus@Will, Freedom, or Cold Turkey* to block distracting websites temporarily. Place your phone out of sight and silence notifications that aren't necessary. By setting specific periods for focused, distraction-free work, you create an environment where you can concentrate fully and work more efficiently.

### 3. The Prioritization Dilemma

Another frequent struggle isn't merely the number of tasks but the difficulty in *determining which tasks truly matter*. Many people end up focusing on immediate but low-impact tasks instead of activities that align with larger goals. Without clear prioritisation, it's easy to get caught up in busy work that doesn't contribute significantly to long-term achievements.

Establish a *weekly review practice* to clarify priorities. At the end of each week, set aside time to look at your upcoming week's tasks and decide which ones align with your larger objectives. Break down larger goals into daily tasks and incorporate them into your schedule. Tools like *Trello, Asana, or Todoist* can help you track tasks, set deadlines, and manage your workload in a way that reflects your priorities.

By addressing your personal time management challenges and integrating these solutions, you'll create a more structured, productive approach to your daily responsibilities, allowing you to accomplish more without feeling overwhelmed.

### 4. Breaking the Cycle of Procrastination

Procrastination is a common hurdle for professionals, often driven by psychological factors like fear, perfectionism, or a lack of motivation. Left unchecked, procrastination can delay progress, increase stress, and reduce the quality of work. Understanding why we procrastinate is key to breaking the habit and building a healthier relationship with time. Procrastination is often rooted in psychological triggers, including fear of failure or perfectionism. When a task feels daunting or overwhelming, our minds naturally try to avoid the discomfort associated with it. Perfectionism can also play a role, as the desire for perfect results can lead us to avoid tasks entirely if we feel unable to achieve our ideal standards. Finally, a lack of motivation may occur when tasks seem uninteresting, difficult, or disconnected from our goals. We will go into this in much more detail later on in the book.

When you understand and recognise procrastination setting in, take a moment to identify the specific reasons behind it. *Ask yourself: What am I avoiding, and why?* Acknowledge these feelings and then reframe the task by connecting it to your larger goals. If you're avoiding a big project, break it down into smaller, achievable steps and set mini-deadlines for each step. Shifting your perspective from "I must do this perfectly" to "I'll make consistent progress" can make the task more approachable.

### 5. Setting Up an Accountability System

*Accountability* is another key component of time management success. When we set goals without any form of accountability, it's easy to let them slide when life gets busy. Having an *accountability system*, whether it's a mentor, a colleague, or even a tracking app, adds a layer of commitment that can help keep you on track.

A good way to stay accountable is to set up weekly check-ins with a colleague or friend who's also working on time management. Alternatively, use tools like *Habitica* or *Streaks* to track progress and celebrate small wins. Checking in with someone or something regularly can motivate you to stick with your time management practices even when the going gets tough.

### 6. Building Time for Reflection

A foundation in time management also involves setting aside time for *self-reflection*. Reflection allows you to assess what's working, what isn't, and where you can improve. Without taking the time to review, adjust, and refine your strategies, it's difficult to make meaningful progress.

If you dedicate just a few minutes each day or week to reflect on your time management habits, it will be time well spent. Ask yourself questions like: What did I accomplish this week? Which strategies worked best? Where did I struggle, and how can I address this going forward? Keeping a time management journal can be an excellent way to track your growth and pinpoint areas where you might need to adjust your approach.

Hopefully, you are now coming to the conclusion that effective time management is a skill that, when implemented properly, can significantly increase productivity and work-life balance.

In this next section, we are going to explore practical techniques and tools that you can use to improve focus, overcome procrastination, audit your time, and set goals that drive meaningful progress. These strategies, when applied consistently, will help you take control of your time and move closer to achieving your professional and personal goals.

## IMPLEMENTING THE POMODORO TECHNIQUE FOR FOCUS

The *Pomodoro Technique* is a proven method for maintaining focus and combating procrastination. It involves working in short, focused intervals of around 25 minutes, followed by a 5-minute break. After completing four Pomodoros (work intervals), you take a longer break (15-30 minutes). This technique is particularly effective for large, overwhelming tasks that feel difficult to start or finish.

To implement the Pomodoro Technique, set a timer for 25 minutes and commit to focusing solely on one task for that period. When the timer goes off, take a 5-minute break to recharge, stretch, walk, grab a drink, or do something that refreshes you. After completing four Pomodoros, take a longer break of 15-30 minutes to give your mind the rest it needs. The Pomodoro Technique builds momentum by creating a sense of urgency and regular, manageable breaks that help prevent burnout.

This structured approach helps break down large, complex tasks into smaller, more achievable chunks, making it easier to focus and maintain motivation throughout the day.

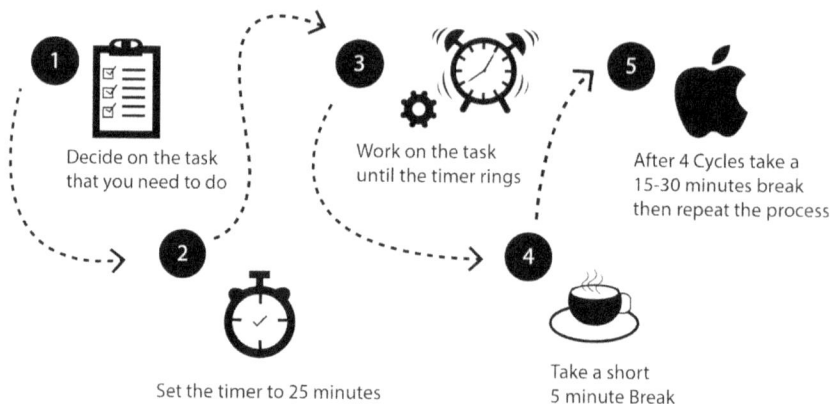

**The Pomodoro Technique**

## Step-by-Step Breakdown:

- Step 1: Choose a Task – Encourages the user to select a specific task to focus on.
- Step 2: Set a Timer for 25 Minutes – Represents the core Pomodoro interval, emphasising commitment to undistracted work.
- Step 3: Work on the Task – Focuses on staying on track during the 25-minute session.
- Step 4: Take a 5-Minute Break – Reinforces the importance of short breaks to rejuvenate and maintain productivity.
- Step 5: After 4 Sessions, Take a Longer Break – Highlights the built-in reward system of the technique, with extended breaks to recharge fully.

## TASK SEGMENTATION: BREAKING DOWN BIG PROJECTS

When faced with large projects, it's easy to feel paralysed by the enormity of the task. The fear of starting something complex can lead to procrastination, and the thought of completing it all at once becomes overwhelming. Breaking down large projects into smaller, manageable tasks can help you build momentum and make the work feel more achievable.

Begin by writing out each component of a project in a logical sequence. Start with tasks that have the least barriers to entry to get the ball rolling. For example, if you're tasked with writing a report, don't start with the introduction. Instead, begin by creating an outline or gathering research. This way, you can build momentum through easy wins that propel you toward the more challenging parts of the project. By focusing on one small step at a time, large projects will seem more manageable, and procrastination will lose its hold on you.

## CONDUCTING A PERSONAL TIME AUDIT FOR ENHANCED CLARITY

A powerful tool for mastering time management is conducting a *time audit*. This process involves tracking your time for a set period, to uncover inefficiencies and to identify patterns in how you allocate your time. A time audit helps you understand where your time is going, which tasks or activities are productive, and where you can make adjustments to improve your focus and productivity.

To begin your time audit, choose a method that works best for you. You can use a simple journal, a spreadsheet, or a *time-tracking app* like *Toggl* or *Clockify* to record your activities. Track everything from work-related tasks to personal downtime for an entire week. The more detailed you are, the more insights you'll gain about your time usage.

Track your activities in 15-30 minute increments. Include everything, from meetings and phone calls to breaks, meals, and distractions. At the end of the week, you'll have a comprehensive snapshot of how you've spent your time. This data will serve as the foundation for making informed decisions about how to optimise your schedule moving forward.

Once your time audit is complete, the next step is to analyse the data to uncover patterns. Identify activities that consume time without adding value, such as excessive social media use, unnecessary meetings, or frequent email checking. In contrast, recognise high-value tasks, those that directly contribute to your personal or professional goals.

Calculate the percentage of time spent on productive versus non-productive activities. Aim to reduce time spent on low-value tasks by a manageable percentage each week. Use this insight to adjust your schedule and ensure your time is spent on activities that align with your priorities.

Once you have the data from your time audit in hand, it's time to make adjustments. Based on the insights gathered, create *"time blocks"* during your most productive hours (usually mornings or periods when you're most alert) to focus on high-priority tasks. Time blocking involves dedicating uninterrupted periods to focused work and minimising distractions during those blocks.

Start by setting aside small blocks of time each day for important, high-value tasks. Gradually increase the length of these blocks as you become more accustomed to uninterrupted work. Balance these productive periods with breaks and leisure activities to avoid

## CRAFTING SMART GOALS TO DRIVE FOCUS AND RESULTS

Setting goals is essential to time management success. Without clear goals, it's easy to become distracted and veer off course.

*SMART goals (Specific, Measurable, Achievable, Relevant, and Time-bound)* offer a structured framework to create goals that are both actionable and motivating. SMART goals help you prioritise effectively, track your progress, and focus on what matters most.

### Using SMART Goals to Build Structure

The SMART criteria provide a simple yet powerful way to create effective goals:

- **Specific:** Define your goal clearly. What exactly do you want to achieve?
- **Measurable:** Ensure that you can track (Measure) progress toward your goal.
- **Achievable:** Make sure the goal is realistic and attainable within your resources.
- **Relevant:** Align your goal with your broader personal or professional objectives.
- **Time-bound:** Set a clear deadline to prevent procrastination and maintain focus.

A good idea is to write down your top three goals for the week, month, or day. For each goal, ensure it meets the SMART criteria to guarantee that it's clearly defined and achievable. Having goals that are both specific and measurable makes it easier to keep focused on the goal and stay motivated.

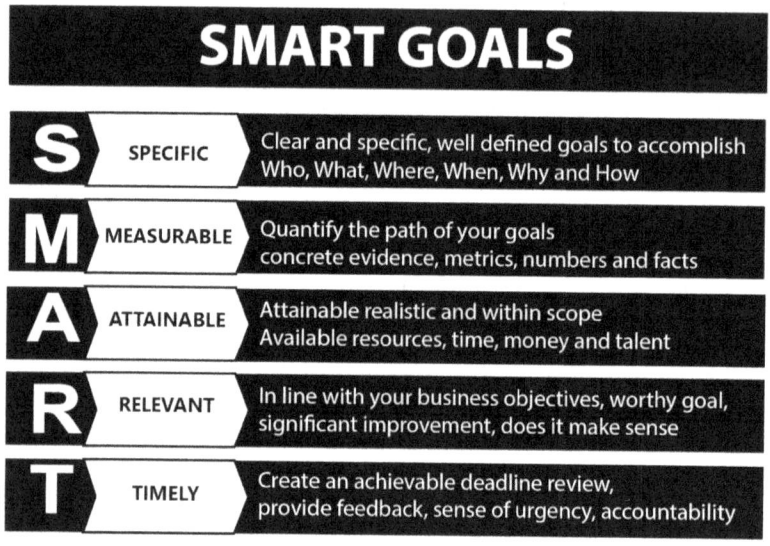

SMART Goals/Objectives

*Tracking and Adjusting Goals*

Setting goals is only half the battle. To stay on track and ensure you're making progress, it's essential to *track your goals regularly*. Using a goal-setting worksheet or *tracking charts* can help you monitor your progress and identify any adjustments that might be needed.

At the end of each week, review your goals to assess whether you're on track. Celebrate small wins and make any necessary adjustments to your strategies. If a goal no longer seems relevant, don't hesitate to revise or pivot it. Regularly assessing your goals ensures that your efforts are aligned with what matters most and helps you stay focused on continuous improvement.

## IDENTIFYING YOUR PEAK PRODUCTIVITY HOURS

Knowing when you're naturally most productive can significantly improve your ability to manage your time effectively. Understanding your personal productivity rhythms allows you to schedule the most demanding tasks during your peak hours, ensuring maximum focus and energy. This awareness is key to making the most of your workday. This is a key component of effective time management. Not all hours are created equal, and finding your personal peak productivity windows can make a world of difference in optimising your focus and task completion. Everyone has distinct energy patterns based on their unique rhythms and aligning your schedule with these natural cycles will allow you to work more efficiently.

**The Science of Circadian Rhythms**

Circadian rhythms are the natural, internal processes that regulate your sleep-wake cycle over a 24-hour period. These rhythms influence your energy levels, focus, and alertness throughout the day. Some people are naturally "morning people" who feel most energised in the early hours, while others are "night owls" who perform better in the evening. It is, therefore, important to identify your Peak Productivity Hours.

The Circadian Rhythm

The diagram above is divided into primary segments representing critical events in the circadian rhythm:

- Wake Up: Typically early morning, when cortisol levels rise and Melatonin secretion stops, signalling the body to become alert and start the day.
- Peak Alertness: Mid-morning to early afternoon, when cognitive functions and focus are at their highest.
- Best Coordination: Often occurring mid-afternoon, when physical performance, especially motor skills, is optimised.

- Melatonin Secretion: Beginning in the evening, this process signals the body to prepare for rest and regulates sleep-wake cycles.
- Deep Sleep: Typically occurring in the late-night hours, critical for physical recovery and mental processing.

*Circadian Rhythms and Their Importance*

- Biological Significance: Circadian rhythms are controlled by the suprachiasmatic nucleus (SCN) in the brain, which responds to light cues from the environment. These rhythms regulate critical processes like sleep, hormone release, digestion, and cognitive function.
- Practical Applications:
  - Sleep Optimisation: Understanding when melatonin secretion begins and when deep sleep occurs helps individuals plan healthy sleep schedules.
  - Peak Productivity: Identifying times of peak alertness and best coordination can help optimise work or physical activities.
  - Health Impacts: Disruptions in circadian rhythms, such as those caused by irregular schedules, jet lag, or shift work, can lead to fatigue, mood disorders, and chronic health issues.

*Identifying Your Peak Productivity Hours*

To identify your peak productivity hours, keep a simple log for a week, rating your focus and energy levels at different intervals throughout the day (morning, afternoon, and evening). Over time, you'll notice patterns that reveal your personal productivity peaks. By scheduling your most challenging tasks during these optimal windows, you'll maximise your output and minimise distractions.

You can align your tasks with your energy levels once you've identified your peak productivity hours, and it's crucial to align your most demanding tasks with these times. For example, if you're most focused in the morning, tackle complex, high-priority tasks during this period, such as deep work, creative brainstorming, or strategic planning. Later in the day, when your energy might dip, you can reserve lighter tasks, such as checking emails, administrative work, or meetings that require less mental intensity.

**Peak Productivity Log**

A simple way to note your productivity is to take a sheet of A4 size paper and break it down into the following key sections and there you have a simple Peak Productivity Log:

- **Date**: A dedicated space at the top for you to record the date, ensuring daily tracking of productivity patterns.
- **Time of Peak Productivity**: Allows you to note the specific time periods when you felt most productive during the day, helping identify recurring patterns or optimal work hours.
- **Tasks Accomplished**: A structured area to list tasks completed during the peak productivity period, offering a clear overview of achievements.
- **Energy Level** (1-10): A simple numerical scale for you to rank your energy levels during your most productive time, enabling you to correlate energy with productivity.
- **Reflections/Notes**: A freeform section for insights, thoughts, or factors that influenced productivity, such as mood, environment, or interruptions.

### Managing Afternoon Slumps

It's not uncommon to experience a drop in energy, particularly after lunch. Known as the "afternoon slump," this period can make staying productive more difficult. However, recognising this challenge in advance allows you to manage your energy better throughout the day.

To combat afternoon fatigue, you can use brief strategies such as a quick walk, stretching, or a mindfulness exercise to recharge your mental focus. Also, prioritise lighter tasks during this time. These activities are less draining, allowing you to continue being productive even when you're not at your peak energy.

So, in summary, build your schedule around your natural productivity ebbs and flows. Time-block your calendar to dedicate high-focus tasks during peak periods and leave low-energy tasks for times when your focus isn't at its best. Harness your energy to work smarter, not harder. Recognising your peak hours can drastically improve both productivity and the quality of your work, leading to more efficient, less stressful days. This simple strategy can help you maintain consistent productivity without over-exerting yourself.

## THE POWER OF SAYING NO: PROTECTING YOUR TIME

In our fast-paced world, there's an ever-present pressure to say "yes" to new commitments, whether at work or in our personal lives. While helping others and embracing new opportunities can be rewarding, it's essential to know when to protect your time. Over-committing or spreading yourself too thin can lead to burnout and hinder your ability to focus on your core priorities.

### The Fear of Missing Out (FOMO)

Fear of missing out (FOMO) is a common motivator that drives us to say yes to everything that comes our way. It might be a new work project, a networking opportunity, or even a social event. However, these distractions can divert your focus from the most critical tasks that align with your long-term goals.

You can combat FOMO by evaluating every new commitment through the lens of your larger objectives. Before agreeing to something new, pause and ask: *Does this opportunity move me closer to my goals? Does it align with my current priorities?* By filtering out requests that don't serve your greater purpose, you can conserve your time and energy for what truly matters.

1. Limit yourself from using social media.
2. Never compare yourself with other's lives.
3. Minimise your distractions by turning your phone off.
4. Do things that matter to you. Switch to enjoying your current lifestyle than updating it online.
5. Keep in mind that "YOU CANNOT DO IT ALL" You cannot be in two places at once.

**Fear of Missing Out (FOMO)**

You have to *set boundaries*. It's an essential part of effective time management. Saying no is not about being unkind; it's about protecting your time, mental space, and energy. When you set clear boundaries, you're ensuring that you can focus on what truly aligns with your values and priorities.

Learn to say no politely but firmly without over-explaining yourself. If appropriate, offer alternatives, like suggesting someone else for the task or proposing a later time. Practice assertiveness when setting boundaries. Setting these boundaries will help you protect your energy and remain focused on your high-priority tasks.

**Saying Yes to Yourself: Prioritising Self-Care**

When we are so busy and where demands are constant, it's easy to neglect your own well-being. However, prioritising self-care is essential for sustaining high productivity and maintaining a healthy work-life balance. Self-care isn't just about taking occasional breaks, it's about weaving it into your daily routine to improve focus, energy, and long-term success.

It's so important to block out time for self-care and treat it with the same priority as any work task. This might include activities like *exercise, reading, taking breaks, or even getting proper sleep*. Remember, when you nurture your physical and mental health, you replenish your energy and become more productive in your professional and personal life. Learn to say no, and importantly, yes to the right things.

## THE ROLE OF ACCOUNTABILITY IN TIME MANAGEMENT

Time management is more than just implementing the right strategies; it's about being accountable to your goals and commitments. Having accountability systems in place can serve as a powerful motivator, helping you stay on track and ensuring consistent progress toward your objectives.

### Setting Up an Accountability System

A structured accountability system can significantly boost your chances of success. Whether it's a *friend, colleague, mentor, or coach*, having someone who checks in on your progress can help keep you motivated and focused.

Firstly, choose an *accountability partner* who shares similar goals. Schedule regular check-ins to review progress, discuss any challenges, and adjust targets. The knowledge that you'll have to report your progress can be a powerful motivator to maintain consistent effort.

### Using Technology for Self-Accountability

The digital age has produced numerous tools which are available to support your accountability efforts. Apps like *Habitica, Stickk,* or *Coach.me*, leverage and encourage consistency in achieving your goals. These tools can track progress, send reminders, and offer rewards for accomplishments, making the process of accountability more engaging.

If you decide on this tool, select an app or tool that aligns with your personal preferences. Set up reminders to keep you on track and motivate you to take consistent action. The key is to find a system that helps you stay focused without overwhelming you.

### Internal Accountability: Self-Reflection and Mindfulness

While external accountability can be helpful, *internal accountability* is equally crucial. It involves being mindful of how you're using your time, *reflecting on your actions*, and holding yourself responsible for your progress. If you are more introverted than extroverted, you may wish to choose this option.

At the end of each day, take 5–10 minutes to reflect on what you have accomplished and where you can improve. Celebrate your wins, no matter how small, and make adjustments for areas where you fell short. This practice of self-reflection helps you stay focused on your long-term goals and encourages a sense of ownership over your time and success.

*Reviewing and Refining Your Time Management System*

Just like any other skill, time management improves with regular review and refinement. As your life and priorities evolve, it's essential to continually evaluate and adjust your system to stay aligned with your goals.

No system is perfect forever, therefore, regularly reviewing your time management system will help you identify inefficiencies, refine your strategies, and ensure that your approach is still working for you. Set aside time each week or month to review your progress, assess your priorities, and make adjustments as necessary.

Schedule regular review periods, whether weekly or monthly, to assess your progress. Use this time to adjust your approach, find areas for improvement, and re-align your strategies with any new goals or priorities. This process of continuous improvement will help you optimise your system for better results.

*Continuous Improvement: The Kaizen Approach*

The *Kaizen* approach is a Japanese concept meaning "continuous improvement." It focuses on making small, consistent, and incremental changes that collectively lead to significant progress over time. Originating in Japanese manufacturing, Kaizen has since been widely adopted in business, personal development, and time management practices globally.

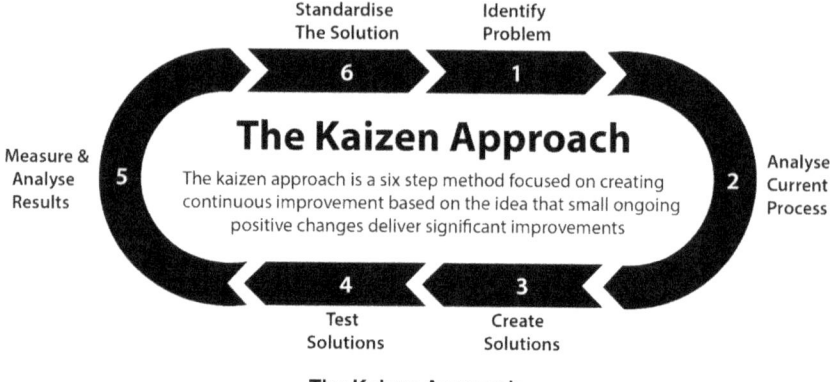

The Kaizen Approach

Key principles of Kaizen include:

1. **Continuous Improvement**: Rather than aiming for big changes, Kaizen emphasises making small, steady improvements that accumulate into substantial long-term gains.
2. **Employee Involvement**: In the workplace, Kaizen encourages input from all employees, valuing insights from every level of an organisation to identify areas for improvement.
3. **Focus on Process**: Kaizen prioritises refining processes rather than solely focusing on outcomes. By improving processes, outcomes naturally improve as well.
4. **Waste Reduction**: A significant aspect of Kaizen is eliminating unnecessary steps or resources, which leads to greater efficiency and less wasted effort.
5. **Standardisation**: Successful improvements become part of standard practice, ensuring that positive changes are maintained over time.

Kaizen can be applied in daily life by making small changes to routines, setting incremental goals, or adjusting workflows to improve productivity and well-being. Applying the *Kaizen philosophy* of continuous improvement by making small, incremental changes over time to optimise your productivity means these minor adjustments can continuously refine your time management system and increase your efficiency.

In your own routine, look for opportunities to improve each week. These improvements can be small, like refining your to-do list, trying a new productivity tool, or altering how you structure your day, but over time, they can compound into significant improvements.

## FLEXIBILITY AND ADAPTATION: THE KEY TO SUSTAINABILITY

It's essential to remain *flexible* in your time management approach. Life will always present unexpected challenges, and your system needs to adapt to maintain productivity and balance.

With this in mind, build 'buffer time' into your schedule for unexpected tasks. When life throws challenges your way, instead of feeling stressed, see it as an opportunity to adjust and adapt your approach.

Reviewing and refining your time management system ensures that you're not just following a set of rules but creating a dynamic system that grows with you. By committing to continuous improvement and staying flexible, you can achieve lasting success in managing your time effectively.

2

# MASTERING YOUR MIND SET
## OVERCOMING TIME MANAGEMENT BARRIERS

In Chapter 1, we discussed how effective time management is not just about tools and systems but about cultivating habits that enable you to make the best use of your time. However, there is another crucial aspect of time management that often goes unaddressed: your *mind set*. Without the right mind set, even the best time management strategies will fall short. Your thoughts, beliefs, and attitudes about time can either propel you forward or hold you back.

In this chapter, we will explore the mental and emotional barriers to effective time management and provide actionable strategies to overcome them. By developing a mind set that supports productivity, efficiency and long-term success, you'll be equipped to break through these barriers and achieve your goals.

### THE IMPACT OF MIND SET ON TIME MANAGEMENT

*Mind set* is the foundation for everything you do, including how you approach time management. Your mind set influences how you perceive tasks, how you handle setbacks, and how motivated you feel to use your time wisely. When your mind set is misaligned with your time management goals, even the most effective systems and techniques won't make a lasting impact.

Carol Dweck's ground breaking work on mind set highlights two key types: *fixed and growth.* A *growth mind set* is the belief that your abilities, including your time management skills, can be developed through effort, learning, and perseverance. When you embrace a growth mind set, you see challenges as opportunities, failures as feedback, and setbacks as a natural part of the learning process. Time management becomes a skill you can hone with practice and you view each attempt as a step toward improvement.

In contrast, a *fixed mind set* suggests that your abilities are predetermined and cannot change. People with a fixed mind set may feel they are either "good" or "bad" at time management, and this belief can prevent them from trying new strategies or improving. For example, someone with a fixed mind set might think, "I'm not disciplined enough to manage my time well" or "I'll never be able to balance everything." Such beliefs can create a self-fulfilling prophecy, where they give up on improving before they even start.

*Shifting from a fixed to a growth mind set is key to overcoming barriers like procrastination, perfectionism, and fear of failure,* issues we'll explore later in the chapter. If you can start viewing time management as a skill that you can grow, you're already on the path to success.

## OVERCOMING PROCRASTINATION

Procrastination is one of the most common barriers to effective time management. We've all put off tasks, opting instead for easier, more enjoyable activities. But procrastination isn't simply laziness; it's often a symptom of underlying fears, anxieties, or perfectionism. Understanding the root causes of procrastination is the first step toward overcoming it.

One major reason we procrastinate is *feeling overwhelmed* by the scale of a task. When faced with a big project, it can be difficult to know where to begin, leading to a sense of paralysis. The solution? Break the task down into smaller, manageable steps. Instead of looking at an entire report and thinking, "I have to write a 10-page report," focus on one small section at a time, such as writing the introduction or outlining the key points. Taking small steps makes the task seem more achievable and reduces the overwhelming feeling that often causes procrastination. Each completed step boosts your sense of accomplishment, motivating you to continue.

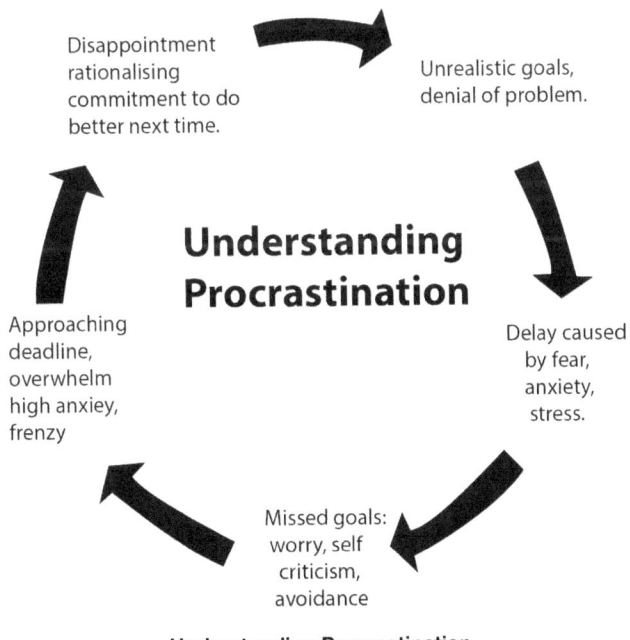

Understanding Procrastination

Another common reason for procrastination is the *fear of failure or imperfection*. We may delay starting a task because we're afraid the outcome won't meet our own standards. To combat this, try the *Five-Minute Rule*: Commit to working on a task for just five minutes. Once you begin, you'll likely find that it's easier to keep going. Even if you don't feel motivated, just getting started is often the hardest part.

*Distractions* also contribute to procrastination. To minimise them, create a *distraction-free workspace* by eliminating clutter and turning off notifications. Consider using time blocking or productivity apps that limit access to distracting websites during designated work periods. This will help you stay focused and reduce the temptation to procrastinate.

Finally, consider *accountability*. Share your goals with someone who will check in on your progress, creating an external pressure on you to follow through. Knowing that someone else is expecting progress can be a powerful motivator to combat procrastination.

### BATTLING PERFECTIONISM

*Perfectionism* can be a significant roadblock to effective time management. While setting high standards for yourself is commendable, striving for perfection can cause delays, stress, and burnout. The key to overcoming perfectionism is to shift your focus from trying to achieve flawlessness to emphasising progress and efficiency.

One way to combat perfectionism is to embrace the concept of *"good enough."* Many tasks don't require perfection and focusing on every minute detail can actually detract from your overall productivity. Instead, aim to complete tasks to the best of your ability within a reasonable time frame. Perfectionism often keeps you from moving forward, while focusing on progress ensures you stay productive.

Another strategy is to apply the *80/20 Rule (the Pareto Principle)*, which asserts that 80% of the results come from just 20% of the effort. In terms of time management, this means that you should focus on the most important aspects of a task, those that will provide the greatest value while leaving less critical details for later. For example, in writing a report, the first draft doesn't need to be perfect; focus on structure and key points, and save fine-tuning for the editing phase.

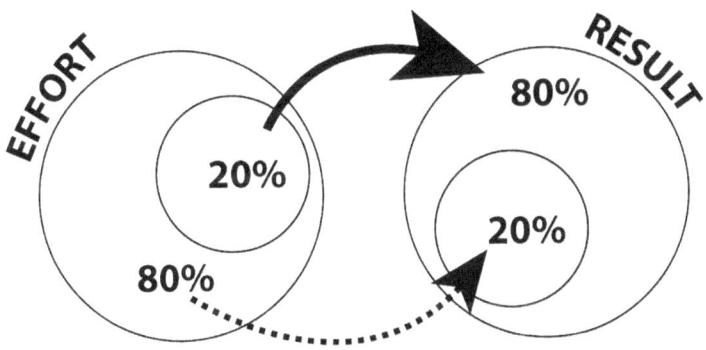

In business, focusing on high impact activities can generate better outcomes. A small number of key actions often produce the majority of results.

**The Pareto Principle**

*Setting time limits* for tasks is another effective way to curb perfectionism. Decide in advance how long you will spend on a task (e.g. 30 minutes for drafting an email or reviewing a report). This forces you to move forward without getting stuck in unnecessary details, allowing you to stay productive while avoiding perfectionism.

## MANAGING FEAR OF FAILURE

Fear of failure is one of the most pervasive mental barriers to time management. The thought of failing can prevent you from taking risks, avoiding important tasks, or giving up altogether when faced with challenges. However, failure is a natural part of the learning process and should not be viewed as a catastrophic event. Understanding how to manage fear of failure is essential for overcoming time management obstacles and moving toward success.

Start by *reframing your thoughts* about failure. Instead of seeing failure as a reflection of your worth or ability, view it as a stepping stone for growth. Each failure provides valuable feedback that can help you improve. Ask yourself, "What can I learn from this experience?" and use that insight to adjust your approach moving forward.

*Visualisation* is another powerful tool to reduce fear of failure. Take a few moments to imagine yourself successfully completing a task, whether it's finishing a project, delivering a presentation, or meeting a deadline. Visualising positive outcomes can help reduce anxiety, increase confidence, and make the task feel less daunting.

Finally, start by taking small, manageable risks. Rather than jumping into a large, intimidating project, begin with smaller tasks that challenge you just enough to step outside your comfort zone. With each success, you'll build confidence, reduce fear, and strengthen your resilience. As you prove to yourself that you can handle challenges, your fear of failure will diminish, making it easier to stay on track and manage your time effectively.

By mastering your mind set and addressing barriers such as procrastination, perfectionism, and fear of failure, you'll be better equipped to manage your time effectively. Embrace the journey of self-improvement, and you'll find that time management becomes a skill that supports your personal and professional success.

## THE ROLE OF SELF-COMPASSION

Effective time management is not only about pushing yourself to be more disciplined or productive; it's also about taking care of your mental and emotional well-being. If you're constantly striving for success and demanding perfection, it's easy to forget the importance of *self-compassion*. Without this crucial element, you risk burnout, stress, and feelings of inadequacy.

Self-compassion is the practice of treating yourself with kindness and understanding, particularly when things do not go as planned. It is essential for staying motivated and resilient as you manage your time and achieve your goals.

To practise self-compassion, treat yourself with the same understanding you would offer to a friend facing a tough situation. When you make a mistake or encounter a setback, instead of criticising yourself, acknowledge that these experiences are part of the learning process. Recognize what you can do differently next time but avoid the trap of excessive self-criticism. Acknowledge your imperfection, reflect on lessons learned, and move forward with a sense of kindness toward yourself. This approach helps you stay motivated, prevent burnout, and sustain a healthy balance between productivity and self-care.

Mindfulness, as has already been discussed, is another tool that can enhance your self-compassion practice. It encourages you to stay present in the moment, instead of ruminating on past mistakes or worrying about future challenges. Mindfulness allows you to let go of negative thoughts that can undermine your focus and energy. Practices like deep breathing, meditation, or journaling help you remain centred, reducing stress and enabling you to nurture a positive relationship with your time.

## DEVELOPING DISCIPLINE AND CONSISTENCY

*Discipline* is essential for achieving long-term success with time management. Without discipline, even the best time management tools will not work. Discipline involves doing what needs to be done, even when you don't feel like it, and sticking to your goals over time, regardless of external distractions or challenges.

The key to developing discipline is *consistency.* Creating small, achievable habits that fit into your daily routine can gradually lead to significant improvements in your time management. Start small by committing to a simple goal, such as dedicating 30 minutes each morning to focused work or setting aside time the night before to plan your day. Over time, these habits will become ingrained and automatic, helping you stay consistent even when motivation is low.

*Accountability* is also an important factor in developing discipline. It can help our conscience keep us on track. Sharing your time management goals with others can increase your commitment to following through. Whether it's a colleague, friend, or mentor, having someone to check in with regularly about your progress can help keep you on track. Knowing that others are expecting you to follow through creates external pressure, which can make it easier to stay disciplined and consistent.

## BUILDING RESILIENCE

Despite your best efforts at planning, life will inevitably present challenges and obstacles. *Resilience* is the ability to bounce back from setbacks and continue moving toward your goals, even when things don't go as planned. Building resilience requires both *mental strength and flexibility,* allowing you to adapt to adversity rather than letting it derail your progress.

One key to building resilience is maintaining a growth mind set. When you face challenges, view them not as insurmountable problems but as opportunities for growth and learning. Instead of asking, "Why is this happening to me?" shift your perspective to "What can I learn from this?" This change in thinking allows you to see each setback as an opportunity to improve your time management and approach.

*Flexibility* is another important component of resilience. Life is unpredictable, and things don't always go according to plan. Being able to adjust your course in response to changing circumstances is crucial for maintaining momentum. If a task takes longer than expected or if unforeseen events force you to change your priorities, be willing to pivot and adjust your plan. Flexibility helps you stay focused on your goals, even when your original plan has to change.

Lastly, *self-care* is a cornerstone of resilience. It's difficult to stay resilient if you're mentally and physically depleted. Building resilience requires maintaining your well-being, which includes proper rest, exercise, and relaxation. Taking care of your body and mind gives you the energy and strength you need to navigate challenges and keep progressing toward your goals.

## CREATING A GROWTH-ORIENTED ENVIRONMENT

Your *environment* plays a significant role in your ability to stay productive, focused, and motivated. To create an environment that supports time management, it's essential to nurture both your *physical* and *psychological spaces.*

Start by organising your *physical workspace.* A cluttered or disorganised environment can lead to distractions, increase stress, and hinder your ability to focus. By creating a clean, organised workspace, you set the stage for increased productivity and reduced stress. Keep essential tools within reach and minimise distractions that may interfere with your focus.

Your *psychological environment* is equally important. Surround yourself with people who inspire, challenge, and support you. Cultivate relationships with mentors, accountability partners, or colleagues who share your values and goals. When you're in an environment that fosters growth and productivity, it becomes easier to stay motivated and maintain momentum toward your goals.

Additionally, immerse yourself in *resources that promote growth and learning.* Books, podcasts, online courses, and communities can provide new ideas, tools, and strategies that can help you refine your time management skills. By engaging with content that supports your personal and professional development, you'll constantly have fresh insights to apply to your time management practices.

Creating a growth-oriented environment encourages you to think beyond your immediate tasks and focus on long-term development. When you have the right environment in place, both physically and psychologically, you'll be better equipped to manage your time effectively, stay focused on your goals, and achieve greater success.

By embracing self-compassion, developing discipline, building resilience, and fostering a growth-oriented environment, you create a strong foundation for managing your time effectively. These mental and emotional practices support your productivity, motivation and ability to overcome obstacles, ultimately helping you achieve both your personal and professional goals. When your mind set aligns with your time management practices, you'll find that success becomes not just possible, but inevitable.

# 3

# BALANCING WORK AND PERSONAL LIFE

Work-Life Balance

In our technologically interconnected world, achieving a balance between work and personal life has become increasingly challenging. The rise of technology, an unrelenting push for productivity and the multifaceted demands of daily life can leave individuals feeling pulled in numerous directions. In this chapter, we will explore the evolution of work-life balance, clarify common misconceptions, and provide actionable strategies to help you manage your time, energy and well-being more effectively.

## THE EVOLUTION OF WORK-LIFE BALANCE

The concept of work-life balance is not a modern-day phenomenon. In fact, it has evolved significantly over the centuries, shaped by social, economic and technological changes. For much of human history, work was centred on survival. In pre-industrial societies, people worked long hours to meet basic needs and personal time was a rare luxury.

The Industrial Revolution in the 18th and 19th centuries marked a dramatic shift in work patterns. Factories imposed long, gruelling hours, often upwards of 12 hours a day, with minimal time for rest or family. The idea of balancing work with other aspects of life simply didn't exist, work was life and time away from it was scarce. Workers toiled endlessly to earn a living and personal time was often sacrificed in the pursuit of economic survival.

Change began in the late 19th century when labour movements gained traction, advocating for better working conditions, fair wages and reasonable hours. The result was the introduction of the eight-hour workday, along with weekends off, providing workers with more time to focus on family, rest, and personal interests. Despite this progress, women, who were expected to handle domestic duties, still faced significant challenges in achieving any real sense of work-life balance.

The modern notion of work-life balance took clearer shape after World War II. With the post-war economic boom in the 1950s and 1960s, family incomes increased and leisure activities became more accessible. More people were able to spend time away from work and the standard eight-hour workday became more firmly entrenched. However, the 1980s and 1990s introduced new challenges as technology began reshaping the workplace. Email, mobile phones and the internet created new opportunities for workers but also meant they could stay connected to work at all times.

These digital advancements made life more convenient in some ways but also blurred the boundaries between work and personal life. The expectation that employees should be available around the clock emerged, making it more difficult to fully disconnect from work. Fast forward to today and technology continues to influence the dynamics of work-life balance, introducing new flexibility through remote work and digital tools while simultaneously creating greater complexity in how we separate work and personal life.

## DEFINING MODERN WORK-LIFE BALANCE

In the past, achieving work-life balance was often viewed as a matter of simply splitting your time evenly between work and personal life. This "equal split" model is increasingly outdated and unrealistic. In today's world, work-life balance is less about perfection and more about effectively managing your time, energy, and attention to align with your personal values, priorities, and goals.

Modern work-life balance is less about maintaining strict boundaries between work and personal life and more about integrating them in a way that works for you. Rather than viewing work and personal responsibilities as opposing forces that must be kept separate, integration involves allowing these two spheres of life to complement one another. For example, it's about knowing when to focus on work, such as during an important deadline or project and when to switch gears to focus on personal priorities, such as family, health, or hobbies.

This integrated approach provides flexibility and acknowledges that different times in life require different levels of focus. During certain periods, you may need to dedicate more time to work, such as when transitioning into a new role or meeting critical deadlines. Conversely, at other times, you may need to invest more time in personal matters, whether it's caring for a loved one, prioritising self-care, or working on personal development. Achieving work-life balance doesn't mean that your time is always split evenly, but that you are intentional about how you allocate your energy across various responsibilities.

Ultimately, work-life balance is deeply personal. What works for one individual may not work for another and balance will likely look different for you at different stages of your life. It's important to recognize that balance is not a static, one-size-fits-all concept but a dynamic and evolving system that shifts in response to your changing needs, goals, and priorities. The key is to create a system that reflects your own values and circumstances, ensuring that both your professional and personal lives can thrive without one overwhelming the other.

## COMMON MISCONCEPTIONS ABOUT WORK-LIFE BALANCE

There are numerous misconceptions about what achieving work-life balance looks like and these misconceptions can lead to frustration, guilt and burnout. Let's take a look at some of the most common myths:

1. **Balance Means Equal Time Allocation**: One of the biggest myths is that work-life balance requires a 50/50

split between work and personal life. This can lead to stress when it doesn't happen. In reality, some weeks, your work will demand more time and other weeks, your personal life will take precedence. Balance is about making conscious choices based on what matters most at any given time.

2. **Once You Achieve Balance, You're Set**: Another myth is that once you reach balance, everything will fall into place. The reality is that life is dynamic, and so is balance. Circumstances change and you may need to continually adjust your approach. Balance is an ongoing process, not a destination.

3. **Balance Means Doing It All**: Many people feel pressured to "do it all" and be perfect in both their professional and personal lives. This myth leads to burnout and guilt when it's not possible to keep up. True balance is about setting boundaries and focusing on what's truly important rather than trying to fulfil every expectation placed on you.

4. **Balance Is Only About Time Management**: Time management is an important part of work-life balance, but it's not the whole picture. In addition to managing your time, you need to consider how you're managing your energy and emotions. Focusing only on time can lead to a rigid, unfulfilling approach, whereas an energy-conscious approach enables you to feel more energized and focused throughout the day.

5. **Work-Life Balance Means You Never Have to Work Overtime**: Some people believe that achieving work-life balance means they'll never have to work extra hours. While it's true that balance encourages healthier boundaries, there may still be times when you need to work overtime or handle unexpected demands. The key is

to ensure that this is not a regular occurrence and that you're prioritising personal time when possible.

As work-life balance has become such a popular topic, these misconceptions really have to be contextualised. One of the most persistent myths is that achieving balance means giving equal time to both work and personal life. In reality, perfect balance is rarely attainable, nor is it necessary. It's more about making conscious decisions based on your current priorities and goals. Sometimes, work may require more time and energy, while at other times, your personal life may need to take precedence.

Work-life balance is not a one-time achievement rather it is an ongoing process. In truth, balance is a continuous adjustment. Your work-life balance will evolve depending on the circumstances of your life, whether it's career changes, family events, or personal milestones. It's important to recognise that work-life balance is not something you achieve once and for all but something you maintain through mindful and intentional choices.

### STRATEGIES FOR ACHIEVING WORK-LIFE BALANCE

Achieving work-life balance may seem like a daunting task, but with intentional strategies, you can create a harmonious blend of work and personal life. Here are some key strategies to help you manage your time and energy more effectively:

1. **Set Clear Boundaries**: While integration is important, establishing boundaries is essential for maintaining your well-being. Decide when you will and won't work, such as setting specific hours for work and designating certain times for personal activities. This ensures that you create time for both without the two interfering with each other.

2. **Prioritise Tasks Based on Values**: Your values and goals should dictate how you allocate your time. Identify what truly matters to you, whether it's advancing your career, spending time with family, or focusing on your health. Use these priorities to help guide decisions about where to invest your time and energy.
3. **Use Technology Wisely**: Leverage technology to enhance your productivity and create more flexibility in your work schedule. Tools like *project management software, task lists, and calendar apps* can help you stay organised, while *communication tools* allow for remote work and reduced commute time. However, be mindful of overuse and ensure you set boundaries for when and how you use technology.
4. **Practice Time Blocking**: Time blocking involves setting aside specific chunks of time for specific tasks. This helps you ensure that both work and personal tasks receive the attention they deserve. For example, you might block off mornings for focused work and evenings for family time or self-care.
5. **Learn to Say No**: Overcommitting is one of the biggest obstacles to achieving work-life balance. Be mindful of your limits and practice saying no to tasks or responsibilities that do not align with your priorities. Learning to say no will help you preserve time for the things that matter most.
6. **Take Breaks and Prioritise Self-Care**: Regular breaks throughout the day are essential for maintaining focus and energy. Use your breaks to recharge, whether by taking a walk, meditating, or simply stepping away from your workspace. Prioritising self-care helps prevent burnout and ensures that you are physically and mentally prepared to tackle both work and personal responsibilities.

Achieving work-life balance is not a destination but an ongoing journey. It requires intentionality, flexibility, and a willingness to adjust as your circumstances change. By understanding the evolution of work-life balance, recognising common myths and implementing practical strategies, you can create a life where both your professional and personal pursuits coexist in harmony. It's not about perfection, it's about designing a lifestyle that supports your goals, values and well-being. Balancing work and life is an ongoing process of evaluation and adjustment, but with the right mind set and tools, you can find a rhythm that works for you.

HOW TO DEFINE YOUR OWN WORK-LIFE BALANCE

Since work-life balance is personal and subjective, it's essential to define what it looks like for you. Without a clear understanding of your own values, goals and needs, it can be challenging to make conscious choices about how to allocate your time effectively. Here are steps to help you define and maintain your own balance:

1. **Reflect on Your Values**

The foundation of achieving work-life balance is understanding what matters most to you. Reflect on your core values, whether it's family, career growth, health, or personal development. Knowing your values will provide clarity on what you need to prioritise. For example, if family is your top priority, you may decide that no matter how busy your work gets, you will carve out time for dinner with loved ones. This will serve as the basis for how you manage your time and energy. Take a moment to reflect on what matters most in your life. Do you value family time above all else? Is career advancement your top priority? Are health and fitness non-negotiable? Understanding your values is the foundation of creating balance. Write them down and consider how each area of your life aligns with these values.

## 2. Assess Your Current Situation

Take an honest look at how you're currently spending your time. Keep a time journal for a week or two to see where your hours are going. Are you spending too much time at work or on non-essential tasks? Are there areas of your life that you're neglecting? This exercise can reveal how closely your current routines align with your values and where you might need to adjust. It will also help you see where you're overcommitting or saying "yes" to things that don't reflect your priorities and values.

## 3. Set Clear Priorities

Once you've identified what matters most to you, set clear priorities for your personal and professional life. Consider what needs to be addressed first, and let that guide your decisions. For instance, if you value health and fitness, prioritise time for exercise or healthy meals. If your career is a key focus, you might allocate more time for professional development. Clear priorities will help you make decisions more easily, allowing you to dedicate your time and energy to what matters most. These priorities will serve as a guide for how you make decisions about where to invest your time and energy. For example, if spending time with family is a priority, you might block out family dinners in your schedule before agreeing to work late.

## 4. Design Your Ideal Day or Week

After reflecting on your values and setting priorities, create a daily or weekly schedule that incorporates both work and personal responsibilities. *Time blocking* can be a powerful tool here, as it allows you to allocate specific blocks of time to work tasks, personal commitments, and self-care. It can help you achieve this by scheduling specific times for different tasks, ensuring that both work and personal responsibilities are covered without encroaching on each other. For example, you might set aside the mornings for focused work, afternoons for meetings, and evenings for personal activities. The goal is to design a routine that enables you to manage both work and life without letting one encroach on the other. Start by designing a daily or weekly routine that reflects your values and priorities. Make sure you carve out time for both work and personal activities.

5. **Adjust and Adapt**

Work-life balance is not a static concept. Your priorities, work demands, and personal circumstances will evolve, and your approach to balance must adapt accordingly. Periodically review your routine and make adjustments as needed. Don't be afraid to make changes if something isn't serving you. This flexibility is essential to maintaining a sustainable and healthy work-life balance over time. Work, personal life and priorities evolve and so should your balance.

## STRATEGIES FOR EFFECTIVE WORK-LIFE INTEGRATION

Achieving work-life integration is about finding ways to blend professional and personal responsibilities in a harmonious and flexible way. It's not about rigid boundaries, but about working in a way that complements all aspects of your life. Here are several strategies to help you integrate work and personal life more effectively:

### 1. Time-Block for Productivity

*Time blocking* is a great way to allocate specific time slots to different activities. By scheduling both work and personal tasks, you can ensure that neither one overtakes the other. For example, block 9 a.m. to 12 p.m. for focused work, take a break for lunch, and then reserve 1 p.m. to 3 p.m. for meetings. Personal tasks like exercise, reading, or family time can be scheduled for the evening or weekends.

### 2. Learn to Say No

Learning to say no is one of the most effective strategies for maintaining work-life balance. If a task or request doesn't align with your values or priorities, don't be afraid to politely decline. Saying yes to everything will only drain your energy and time, leaving you stretched too thin. By setting boundaries and prioritising, you can protect your time for what truly matters.

### 3. Delegate When Possible

*Delegating tasks*, whether at work or home, can help you free up time for higher-priority activities. At work, delegate projects that others can handle. At home, share household responsibilities with family members or outsource tasks, such as cleaning or grocery shopping. Delegating ensures that you're not overwhelmed and helps you focus on what you do best.

### 4. Embrace Remote Work

Remote work offers greater flexibility and eliminates commute time. If your job allows for it, consider working from home or setting up a hybrid schedule. This flexibility can help you balance your work and personal commitments more easily. However, it is important to set boundaries to prevent your work from bleeding into your personal time.

### 5. Take Regular Breaks

Taking *breaks* throughout the day is essential to maintaining focus and preventing burnout. Whether it's a quick walk, a coffee break, or simply stepping away from your desk for a few minutes, breaks help recharge your energy, clear your mind and improve overall productivity.

### 6. Practice Mindfulness and Stress Management

*Stress management* is crucial for maintaining balance. Practices like mindfulness, meditation, and deep breathing exercises can help reduce stress, improve focus, and enhance overall well-being. Taking just a few minutes to practise deep breathing or mindfulness can have a significant impact on your emotional and mental health, supporting a more balanced life.

Achieving and maintaining work-life balance is an ongoing, dynamic process. By redefining what balance means for you, setting clear priorities, and adopting strategies to integrate work and life effectively, you can create a fulfilling and sustainable routine. It's about being intentional, flexible, and adaptable as you navigate the demands of both your professional and personal life.

## TAKING CARE OF YOURSELF

Maintaining a *healthy* work-life balance isn't just about managing time and setting boundaries between your professional and personal life. One of the most crucial elements of achieving balance is *taking care of yourself*. When life becomes busy, it's easy to overlook your physical, emotional, and mental well-being, especially when you're juggling multiple responsibilities. However, neglecting self-care can eventually lead to burnout, decreased productivity and diminished satisfaction in both work and life. Self-care is not an occasional treat or luxury; it's an ongoing practice that ensures you have the energy, resilience, and mental clarity to perform at your best across all areas of life.

In a world that constantly demands more from us, it's easy to neglect our own needs in favour of work or family obligations. However, self-care should never be seen as an afterthought or something you do only when you're feeling depleted. By prioritising self-care and making it a non-negotiable part of your routine, you're ensuring that you have the energy, clarity and resilience to take care of your responsibilities and pursue your goals.

*Physical Health*

Your physical health is the foundation of your overall well-being and plays a significant role in maintaining a productive, balanced life. Taking care of your body through regular exercise, a nutritious diet and sufficient sleep ensures that you have the energy and stamina to meet the demands of both your work and personal life.

- **Exercise:** Regular physical activity is essential for managing stress and enhancing mental clarity. Exercise releases endorphins, the body's natural mood boosters, which can reduce feelings of anxiety and depression. Whether it's a daily walk, yoga session, or a more intense workout, find an activity that you enjoy and make it a non-negotiable part of your routine. Exercise not only

improves your mood but also boosts energy levels and cognitive function, helping you stay sharp and focused throughout the day.
- **Nutrition:** What you eat plays a significant role in your ability to maintain energy levels and mental focus. A balanced diet rich in fruits, vegetables, whole grains, lean proteins and healthy fats provides your body and brain with the nutrients they need to function optimally. Eating nutrient-dense meals also supports your immune system, ensuring you stay healthy and can handle the demands of work and personal commitments. Avoiding excessive caffeine and sugar can also help regulate your energy levels and mood.
- **Sleep:** Never underestimate the importance of quality sleep. Sleep is essential for physical and mental recovery and chronic sleep deprivation can have serious consequences. It can lead to mood swings, irritability, poor decision-making and impaired concentration, all of which can negatively affect your personal and professional life. Aim for 7-9 hours of sleep each night and create a bedtime routine that promotes relaxation, such as limiting screen time and creating a calming sleep environment. Prioritise sleep as much as you would any work or social commitment and make sure it's a non-negotiable part of your daily routine.

*Mental and Emotional Health*

Taking care of your mental and emotional health is just as important as looking after your body. Self-care in this area involves cultivating a positive mind set, reducing stress and maintaining resilience in the face of challenges.

- **Stress Management:** Work and personal life can be overwhelming at times, but managing stress effectively is essential for maintaining balance. Incorporating stress-reduction techniques such as mindfulness, deep breathing, or meditation can help you stay calm and focused, even in high-pressure situations. Taking short breaks during the day to breathe deeply or practise a quick mindfulness exercise can reset your emotional state and boost your productivity. For longer-term stress relief, consider incorporating practices like yoga, Pilates, or journaling into your routine.
- **Mindfulness and Meditation:** Practising mindfulness or meditation can improve your ability to stay present, reduce anxiety and enhance emotional well-being. These practices help you cultivate a calm, centred state of mind, making it easier to navigate the ups and downs of both work and personal life. Even a few minutes of deep breathing or a short meditation session can help reset your mind and reduce emotional tension.
- **Social Connections:** Emotional well-being thrives when you foster meaningful relationships. Taking time to connect with friends, family, or colleagues can provide emotional support, reduce stress and improve your mood. Strong social connections create a sense of belonging and provide opportunities for fun, laughter and relaxation. Whether it's a regular coffee date with a friend or a family outing on the weekend, make sure to prioritise social interactions that nurture your emotional health.

## INCORPORATING BREAKS AND DOWNTIME

In addition to physical and mental health, it's important to integrate regular breaks and downtime into your daily routine. Taking breaks throughout the day allows you to step away from the demands of work and recharge, which in turn helps prevent burnout and maintain focus.

- **Micro-Breaks:** Even just a few minutes away from your desk or workspace can be refreshing. Try incorporating micro-breaks every hour, where you step away from your screen, stretch, or take a walk around the block. These small moments of respite give your brain a chance to reset and help maintain productivity without feeling drained.
- **Longer Breaks:** In addition to micro-breaks, scheduling longer breaks during your day can help you decompress and prevent burnout. A longer lunch break, a walk during the afternoon, or a short nap can all be valuable forms of self-care that allow you to return to work with renewed focus and energy. Use your longer breaks to do something that genuinely recharges you, whether it's connecting with loved ones, reading a book, or engaging in a hobby you enjoy.

## SCHEDULING TIME FOR FUN AND RELAXATION

Self-care also involves making time for activities that bring you joy and relaxation. While work may feel urgent, it's essential to have activities outside of work that help you unwind and have fun. These moments are not indulgences; they're necessary for maintaining balance and well-being.

- **Hobbies and Interests:** Whether it's painting, reading, gardening, or another passion, make sure you set aside time for activities that bring you joy. Hobbies offer an opportunity to disconnect from work and do something that fulfils you outside of your professional obligations.

These activities can help reduce stress, enhance creativity and promote a sense of accomplishment.
- **Socialising and Fun:** Don't forget to prioritise social activities and downtime with friends and family. Laughter and connection are important for emotional well-being and socialising provides an opportunity to recharge and enjoy life outside of work. Whether it's a casual night out with friends or a family gathering, these moments of relaxation and joy are key to maintaining balance.

Remember, self-care isn't just about pampering yourself when things get tough. It's about adopting a mind set that values your well-being and making small, consistent choices that support your physical, mental and emotional health every day. By making self-care a priority, you'll be better equipped to maintain a healthy work-life balance and lead a more fulfilling life.

# MAKE A DIFFERENCE AND GIVE A REVIEW

*"The best way to find yourself is to lose yourself in the service of others."*

— MAHATMA GANDHI

**Your opinion is powerful!**

By sharing your thoughts on *'The Simple Time Management Guide for Professionals'*, you're not just reflecting on your own journey, you're giving others the courage and inspiration to begin theirs.

If this book has helped you gain control of your time, build better habits, or find balance in your busy life, your story could be the light that someone else needs to make a change. Every review is a ripple that reaches someone who is ready to grow, succeed and thrive.

WHY YOUR REVIEW MATTERS:

- **Inspire Others:** Your feedback could be the nudge someone needs to invest in themselves and their future.
- **Share Your Wins:** When you highlight what worked for you, you help others see that success is within their reach.
- **Support the Mission:** Your review spreads the message of Time Management, focus, work-life balance and productivity to more professionals around the world.

HOW TO WRITE A REVIEW:

1. **Be Honest:** Share your favourite parts, key takeaways, or how the book made a difference in your life.
2. **Keep It Simple:** A few sentences about what you loved is all it takes to make an impact.
3. **Post It Online:** Reviews on Amazon or Goodreads are the best way to help others discover this guide.

We love helping others and hope you will do the same. Thank you!

**Freedom Publications**

https://www.amazon.com/review/create-review/?asin=B0DTF27PKW

# 4

# SUSTAINING AND ADAPTING YOUR TIME MANAGEMENT STRATEGIES

Achieving effective time management is not a one-time accomplishment; it's an ongoing process that requires consistent attention and adaptation. Just as an artist chisels away at a block of marble to reveal a masterpiece, time management requires continuous refinement. *The Kaizen philosophy*, focused on incremental, continuous improvement, emphasises this approach, encouraging small, manageable changes that compound over time to produce significant results. With this mind set, you don't need to overhaul your entire routine overnight. Instead, you make gradual, consistent adjustments that help you become more efficient, balanced and productive. Why does Kaizen matter? Because every organisation and individual wants to improve, whether it's to serve better, grow stronger, or make life easier. Improvement isn't a one-time goal; it's a mind set. Kaizen is about asking: *How can we make things better today?*

Kaizen thrives on small, consistent actions. It's not about grand gestures or massive overhauls. Instead, it's about everyone, at every level, making tiny adjustments every day. Through the **Plan-**

**Do-Check-Act (PDCA)** cycle, Kaizen empowers us to try, learn and refine continuously. It's simple: look for opportunities to improve, test an idea, learn from the result, adjust, repeat. When you do this regularly, improvements compound into something amazing. It's not about being perfect. It is about being better than yesterday. That is a purpose worth pursuing.

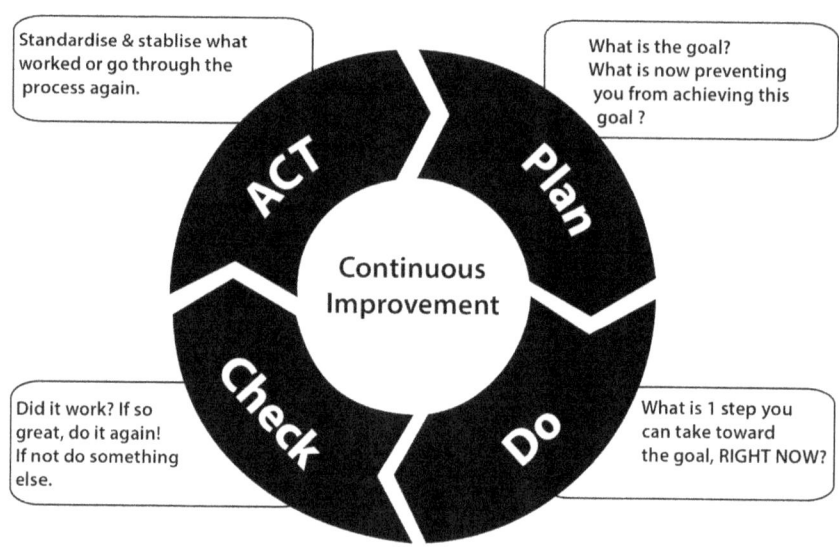

**The PDCA Cycle**

## CONTINUOUS IMPROVEMENT: A LIFELONG JOURNEY

Think of continuous improvement in time-management as tending to a garden. You start with the right seeds, provide the necessary conditions for growth and nurture it regularly. It doesn't happen overnight, but with continuous care, your efforts pay off over time. Similarly, your time management system requires ongoing attention and minor adjustments. The goal is not to reach a perfect state but to maintain progress in small steps. The changes you make today may not yield immediate results, but they will compound over time, transforming your approach to work and life.

Life is dynamic, your goals, responsibilities and circumstances are constantly evolving. So, too, should your time management practices. Continuous improvement is not just about fixing inefficiencies; it's about adopting a mind set that encourages constant growth and adaptation. With this philosophy, you're equipped to evolve as your needs change and as you encounter new challenges and opportunities.

## THE POWER OF SMALL, INCREMENTAL CHANGES

One of the core principles of continuous improvement is making small, incremental changes. These are the building blocks for sustainable success. Unlike drastic changes that may overwhelm or cause resistance, small steps are easier to implement and maintain. They don't require an entire mind set shift or an overhaul of your routine. This approach is particularly empowering for professionals who may feel overwhelmed by the idea of making large, sweeping changes to their time management system.

Small changes have a powerful cumulative effect. They're easier to integrate into your daily life and tend to stick. For example, instead of reworking your entire schedule, start with one manageable change, such as setting aside 30 minutes a day for focused work on a key task. Alternatively, perhaps begin by spending a few minutes each morning reviewing your calendar and prioritising the most important tasks for the day. These small changes will not only improve your productivity but also help you build the momentum needed for larger improvements.

As you continue to make small adjustments, you will start to see the positive impact they have on your productivity. These early successes will motivate you to continue refining your system. Over time, you will build a more effective routine, one small step at a time. This process reinforces the importance of progress over perfection, encouraging you to focus on growth, not immediate perfection.

## SETTING REGULAR REVIEW INTERVALS

For continuous improvement to become a habit, you need to schedule regular check-ins to evaluate your progress. These reviews serve as moments to reflect on your time management strategies and ensure that your practices align with your goals and priorities. The act of reviewing allows you to assess your current situation, identify areas for improvement and celebrate your successes.

Consider setting aside a specific time each week or month to review your time management practices. During these review intervals, ask yourself the following questions:

- Did I meet my goals this week? If not, what caused the delay?
- Which tasks took longer than expected? Was it due to poor planning or an unexpected complication?
- How well did I stick to my prioritised schedule? Were there any distractions or interruptions?
- Are there new tools, strategies, or techniques I could incorporate to improve my efficiency?
- How have I felt emotionally and physically? Have I maintained a healthy balance between work and personal life?

These questions allow you to dig deeper into your time management practices and identify patterns or areas that need refinement. Regular reviews also keep you accountable and allow you to celebrate your progress, reinforcing positive behaviour and encouraging you to stay on track.

## CELEBRATING SUCCESSES AND PLANNING FOR THE FUTURE

It's easy to focus on what's not working, but it's equally important to recognise and celebrate what is. Even small victories, like sticking to a new habit or completing a challenging project, deserve acknowledgment. Celebrating these successes boosts morale and motivation, reinforcing the behaviours that led to your progress. By celebrating these milestones, you strengthen your confidence and encourage yourself to keep moving forward.

Even when things don't go perfectly, celebrating your efforts allows you to build resilience. It reminds you that growth is a journey, not a destination. Recognising your achievements, no matter how small, creates a positive feedback loop that inspires continued action and commitment to improvement.

Celebrating your successes reinforces positive behaviours and fuels continuous motivation. Just as a dog is trained by consistent rewards, recognising milestones in your own journey helps maintain momentum. Celebrations, both personal and collective, reinforce the habits that lead to these successes and create a sense of closure while paving the way for new goals.

**Action Steps:**

- **Personal Celebrations**: Take time to reflect on your achievements, whether through gratitude journaling or simply pausing to acknowledge progress.
- **Group Celebrations**: Celebrate achievements with colleagues, friends, or family to share the joy and build stronger bonds.
- **Set Future Goals**: After celebrating a success, set new goals to keep moving forward. Utilise *vision boards or strategic planning* tools like *SWOT* analysis to create clear, actionable paths for growth.
- **Annual and Quarterly Reviews**: Set aside time annually or quarterly to assess achievements, adjust strategies and plan the next phase of goals.

**Example:**

A student who successfully overcame procrastination celebrated by reflecting on their progress and then set new academic goals. A corporate team that completed a milestone project held a group celebration, recognising the effort of everyone involved, which strengthened teamwork and momentum.

## ADAPTING YOUR STRATEGIES OVER TIME

As you continue to implement small, incremental changes, you may find that your needs evolve, or that certain strategies no longer work as effectively as they once did. This is a natural part of the process. Your goals and priorities will shift over time, and so should your time management practices. This is why continuous improvement is not just a one-time fix, but also a lifelong mind set. You must remain flexible and adapt your strategies as your life and work change.

At times, you may feel frustrated by setbacks or challenges. But remember, continuous improvement is about making steady progress, not about achieving perfection. Every step forward, no matter how small, is a win. Embrace the process of refinement, and understand that time management is not static; it is an ever-evolving practice.

By adopting this approach, you ensure that your time management strategies remain relevant and effective. You will be better prepared to meet new challenges and capitalise on opportunities. As your strategies evolve, so will your productivity, work-life balance and sense of control.

## SEEKING FEEDBACK AND ENGAGING WITH OTHERS

An often overlooked yet powerful strategy for sustaining and adapting your time management practices is seeking feedback from others. While self-reflection is invaluable, it can be difficult to spot areas for improvement on your own. Engaging with colleagues, mentors, or trusted friends can provide fresh perspectives that reveal blind spots you may not have considered. These insights help identify areas where you might be struggling and suggest new techniques or strategies for improving your efficiency. More importantly, seeking feedback from others provides validation and encouragement, which can be especially motivating when you feel uncertain or overwhelmed.

One effective way to incorporate feedback into your continuous improvement process is by forming or joining an *accountability group*. Whether it is a small group of colleagues, a mentor, or a specialized time-management group, these partnerships provide a support structure that can keep you on track. Accountability groups can meet regularly to discuss progress, share tips, track successes, and address challenges. Having an accountability partner or group ensures that you are not navigating the path to better time management alone, and their support can help you remain motivated during moments of difficulty.

In an accountability group, members can celebrate each other's wins, offer constructive feedback and share tips for overcoming obstacles. This sense of community can make the journey toward better time management feel less daunting and provide an additional layer of motivation. Furthermore, being part of a group where you can share your experiences and challenges helps you realize that you are not alone. Everyone faces struggles, but through collective knowledge and encouragement, you will gain new perspectives and refine your strategies. By engaging with others in this way, you gain the reassurance and support needed to continue improving.

## ADAPTING TO CHANGE AND BUILDING RESILIENCE

*Adaptability* is a critical component of continuous improvement. Life is unpredictable, and our ability to adjust to changes is essential for maintaining long-term productivity and achieving success. Whether faced with shifting priorities at work, urgent projects, or personal challenges, the ability to adapt quickly and efficiently is vital for progress. Continuous improvement helps develop this adaptability by providing a mind set and skill set that encourages you to embrace change rather than resist it.

When you embrace continuous improvement, you begin to see challenges and setbacks as opportunities for growth rather than obstacles. Instead of getting discouraged when things do not go as planned, you will be better equipped to reflect, learn and adjust your approach. For example, if you miss a deadline or fail to meet a goal, rather than focusing on the failure itself, take a step back and assess what went wrong. Ask yourself how you can adjust your strategies for future tasks. The goal is not perfection but learning from mistakes and consistently improving your approach to time management.

This adaptability is key to sustaining long-term productivity. In today's fast-paced world, the demands on your time change rapidly. What worked well yesterday might not work as effectively tomorrow. Through continuous improvement, you ensure your time management practices remain flexible and able to adjust in response to new challenges, shifting priorities, and evolving goals. This adaptability helps you stay focused and on track, even as circumstances change. By cultivating resilience through continuous improvement, you can confidently navigate uncertainty and maintain productivity, no matter what comes your way.

## THE ROLE OF ENERGY IN TIME MANAGEMENT

Another essential factor in sustaining your time management strategy is understanding how your energy levels impact your productivity. Time management is not only about managing your time efficiently; it is also about managing your energy. As previously highlighted when discussing Circadian Rhythms, everyone has a unique rhythm to their energy levels throughout the day. Some people are naturally more focused and productive in the morning, while others peak in the afternoon or evening. By aligning your most demanding tasks with your peak energy periods, you can significantly boost your efficiency and make better use of your time.

Recognising your energy patterns allows you to schedule your most important or challenging tasks during the times when you are naturally more alert and focused. For instance, if you're a morning person, it makes sense to tackle critical tasks first thing in the day, when your concentration is at its highest. Conversely, if you find you are more focused in the evening, reserve those late hours for tasks that require deep concentration or creativity.

However, managing your energy isn't just about scheduling tasks. It's also about recognising when your energy is running low and making adjustments to avoid burnout. Overloading yourself with tasks that drain you can lead to exhaustion, reduced productivity and diminished focus.

Just like you schedule breaks to prevent mental fatigue, it's also important to listen to your body and adjust your workload when you feel your energy slipping. Regularly assessing your energy levels and adjusting your schedule to match those fluctuations ensures that you remain productive without overextending yourself.

## CULTIVATING LONG-TERM TIME MANAGEMENT SUCCESS

To sustain and adapt your time management strategies effectively, it's essential to focus on continuous improvement, feedback, adaptability and energy management. By taking a gradual, incremental approach to refinement and engaging with others for feedback and support, you create a resilient, adaptive system that can weather challenges and evolve over time. Adaptability, especially in the face of setbacks or changes, is crucial for maintaining long-term success.

Furthermore, understanding the interplay between time and energy is key to optimizing your productivity and avoiding burnout. Recognise that time management isn't just about fitting more tasks into your day; it's about aligning your energy with your tasks and making conscious choices to sustain your efforts.

By nurturing your time management system with regular feedback, constant adaptation and a mindful approach to your energy, you create a sustainable foundation for success. The process of continuous improvement, combined with these strategies, ensures that you'll remain productive, balanced and prepared for whatever challenges the future may bring.

## THE LIFELONG JOURNEY OF IMPROVEMENT

Therefore, as I have already said, sustaining and adapting your time management strategies is an ongoing journey. With a focus on small, incremental changes, you can avoid burnout, reduce stress and continuously improve your efficiency. By regularly reviewing your practices, celebrating your successes and adapting to new circumstances, you build a time management system that is dynamic and effective.

Remember, time management is not about perfection or rigid routines, it's about progress. Like the sculptor shaping the marble or the gardener tending to their plants, your efforts to improve your time management will yield lasting results if nurtured consistently. Embrace the process and know that every small step forward is part of a larger transformation towards greater productivity, balance and success.

Continuous improvement is a commitment to a lifetime of growth, adaptation, and self-reflection. Your journey toward effective time management doesn't stop after a few small victories. Every day presents an opportunity to learn, adjust, and refine your approach. Challenges should be seen not as obstacles but as stepping stones on the path to improvement. By embracing continuous improvement, you're committing to a life of learning, evolving, and growing, personally and professionally.

The more you practise, the more effective you'll become at managing your time, leading to greater fulfilment and the realisation of your goals. In a world of constant change, your ability to adapt and refine your approach will keep you ahead, enabling you to take full control of your time and your life. Every small change you make, no matter how minor it seems, is a building block that contributes to your larger success. As you continue to apply the principles of continuous improvement, your time management system will evolve to meet your growing needs and support your ambitions.

***Interactive Exercise: Continuous Improvement Journal***

A great way to track your journey of continuous improvement is through a Continuous Improvement Journal. This tool will serve as a powerful resource to track your progress, reflect on the adjustments you've made and document the lessons learned from your time management efforts. Writing regularly in your journal provides you with insights into your growth, highlights areas still needing attention and celebrates victories, big or small.

Your journal doesn't need to follow a rigid structure. It can include reflections on how your day went, feedback from others, insights from review intervals, or any new strategies you want to test. The key is consistency. By maintaining a journal, you'll create a record of your improvement over time and stay motivated to continue making progress, even when the path feels slow.

Remember, progress in time management is not always linear. There may be moments of rapid improvement followed by slower periods. But by revisiting your journal, you'll be able to see how far you've come, adjust your approach if necessary, and stay committed to the process. The journal becomes a powerful motivator and a source of encouragement for your ongoing development.

## CULTIVATING A GROWTH MIND SET FOR PRODUCTIVITY

At the heart of continuous improvement is the concept of a growth mind set, the belief that abilities, skills and intelligence can be developed over time through effort, learning and perseverance. This mind set challenges the idea of fixed abilities and opens up a world of possibilities for growth. When you embrace a growth mind set, each challenge becomes an opportunity to learn and enhance your skills, pushing beyond the limitations you may have once believed to be true.

Consider this scenario: you're standing at the base of a daunting mountain, unsure of whether you can reach the top. A fixed mind set might tell you it's impossible, that the mountain is too high and you're too inexperienced. But a growth mind set encourages you to view the climb as an opportunity for growth, one step at a time. The journey toward productivity and efficiency requires this mind set shift, as it allows you to approach challenges as opportunities for improvement rather than insurmountable barriers.

The benefits of a growth mind set are profound. First, it increases *motivation*. When you believe that effort leads to improvement, you approach tasks with *enthusiasm* and *determination*. The belief that you can grow propels you forward, driving you to keep working toward your goals. Second, it fosters *resilience*. Setbacks are no longer seen as failures, but rather as learning experiences. When you adopt a growth mind set, you're more likely to bounce back from challenges, adapt and persevere. This resilience not only makes you more productive but also improves your overall life experience as you learn to navigate setbacks with optimism.

*Strategies for Cultivating a Growth Mind set*

To effectively cultivate a growth mind set, there are several strategies you can adopt:

1. **Positive Self-Talk**
   - The way you talk to yourself influences your mind set. Replace negative self-talk like, "I can't do this," with positive affirmations such as, "I can learn how to do this." This simple shift helps you focus on growth rather than limitations and nurtures your belief in your ability to improve.
2. **Embrace Failure as a Learning Tool**
   - Failure is an inevitable part of any process. Instead of viewing it as a setback, use it as a learning opportunity. Reflect on what went wrong, what you can improve, and how to approach the task differently next time. By reframing failure in this way, you foster resilience and build adaptability, two crucial elements of both productivity and personal growth.
3. **Seek Challenges and Experiment**
   - When you adopt a growth mind set, you actively seek out challenges. Instead of avoiding difficult tasks, you see them as opportunities to stretch your abilities. Don't be afraid to experiment with new strategies, tools, or techniques and view each experiment as part of your growth journey.
4. **Celebrate Progress, Not Just Results**
   - A growth mind set encourages you to appreciate the journey, not just the destination. Take the time to

acknowledge small victories along the way. Whether it's a task completed ahead of schedule, a productive meeting, or simply a day where you stayed on track, recognising these successes helps reinforce the mind set of continuous improvement.

## REAL-LIFE EXAMPLES OF A GROWTH MIND SET

Many individuals have embodied the principles of a growth mind set and found success through persistence and learning from failures.

Take the example of a young entrepreneur who faced numerous rejections. Rather than giving up, she used each rejection as a learning opportunity, refining her pitch and product offering. Through perseverance and adapting based on feedback, she was able to secure funding and successfully launch her business.

Or consider the story of a person who once struggled with public speaking. Initially, fear and doubt held them back, but by adopting a growth mind set and viewing each speaking opportunity as a chance to improve, they gradually gained confidence and honed their skills. Today, they are a sought-after public speaker, inspiring audiences worldwide with their message of resilience and growth.

These stories illustrate that a growth mind set can transform challenges into opportunities and turn setbacks into stepping stones toward greater success. Cultivating this mind set requires consistent effort, but the results, both in your professional life and personal growth, are well worth it.

## EMBRACE THE POWER OF GROWTH

To cultivate a growth mind set, begin by reflecting on how you view challenges, abilities and setbacks. Are you quick to give up, or do you see difficulties as opportunities for growth? By practising positive self-talk, embracing failure as a tool for learning, and welcoming new challenges, you'll begin to shift your mind set toward growth. Surround yourself with *like-minded individuals* who support and encourage growth, as their influence will help keep you motivated.

By adopting a growth mind set, you unlock your true potential. You will navigate challenges with confidence and resilience, adapt more easily to changes and ultimately increase your productivity. The journey to a more fulfilling, productive life begins with the understanding that challenges are not roadblocks but the very tools that shape your success. Embrace each challenge, cultivate your growth mind set and watch your life and productivity transform.

## THE POWER OF REFLECTION AND SELF-ASSESSMENT

Reflection is vital for effective time management as it enhances self-awareness and helps you fine-tune your habits. It allows you to assess past actions, identify productive patterns and pinpoint areas that need improvement. Through reflective journaling, you can document thoughts, emotions and progress, which leads to valuable insights. Regular self-check-ins are also effective for maintaining clarity on your daily priorities and challenges. These brief introspections ensure your actions align with your goals, keeping you mindful of your growth trajectory.

*Action Steps:*

- **Journal regularly**: Dedicate time to journal about your daily or weekly experiences, identifying recurring habits and emotions tied to time management.
- **Self-check-ins**: Incorporate daily or weekly check-ins by asking: "What went well today?", "What could I improve?", and "How did I feel about my time management?"
- **Monthly Reviews**: Conduct monthly assessments to reflect on larger goals and adjust strategies.

**Example:**

An executive who journaled her daily tasks noticed time drains and learned to delegate better, improving productivity and well-being. A student used self-check-ins to recognize procrastination triggers, leading to focused time management strategies that enhanced performance.

## INTEGRATION WITH BROADER PRACTICES

These strategies, reflection, celebration and planning, are interconnected with continuous improvement and a growth mind set, creating a holistic approach to personal and professional development. Regularly celebrating small victories while assessing progress and setting goals ensures sustained motivation, resilience and clarity on the path ahead.

By integrating reflection into your daily and monthly routine and by consciously celebrating successes and planning for the future, you foster an environment where continuous growth is both achievable and fulfilling.

# 5

# MASTERING THE ART OF DELEGATION FOR BETTER TIME MANAGEMENT

Picture a juggler at the height of their performance. Their arms move with fluid precision, tossing one ball into the air, catching another, all while keeping their eyes trained on the rhythm of the act. However, as impressive as this performance may seem, it's easy to forget that there is one crucial skill behind the juggler's success, i.e. knowing when to let go of a ball. It's not just about skilfully managing everything at once, it's about recognising when to delegate, when to pass something off and when to trust someone else to carry the load.

Mastering the art of delegation is one of the most powerful yet often overlooked strategies for effective time management. In the context of time management, delegation involves sharing tasks, responsibilities and decisions with others in order to free up your own time and focus on what matters most. It's not just about reducing your workload, it's about leveraging the strengths and capabilities of others to help you achieve your goals more efficiently.

While the concept of delegation may seem like a simple one, many people struggle with it. It's easy to fall into the trap of thinking that no one can do things as well as you can, or that taking the time to delegate will be more work than it's worth. However, effective delegation can be a game-changer for your productivity and your overall time management. Like a skilled juggler, knowing when to release a ball is just as important as keeping others in motion. Delegation is a powerful tool that frees up your time, leverages the strengths of others, and enables you to focus on what truly matters.

## THE PSYCHOLOGY OF DELEGATION: LETTING GO OF CONTROL

One of the biggest obstacles to effective delegation is the fear of losing control. Many individuals, especially those in leadership positions or those who are highly detail-oriented, struggle with the idea of handing over a task to someone else. There's often an underlying belief that if you want something done right, you have to do it yourself. But this mind set is not only counterproductive; it can also lead to burnout. By holding on to too many responsibilities, you can quickly become overwhelmed, leaving little energy or time for the work that truly requires your focus.

To delegate effectively, it's crucial to first examine your relationship with control. Why are you hesitant to let go? Often, this stems from a fear that the task won't be done to your standards, or that you'll have to invest more time in overseeing someone else's work. However, when you shift your focus from doing everything yourself to empowering others to help, you unlock a powerful resource, *trust*. Trusting others not only frees up your time, but it also fosters a sense of collaboration and teamwork. It's important to remember that delegation doesn't mean abdicating responsibility, it means sharing the workload in a way that plays to everyone's strengths, ultimately helping you, (or others, if you are working in a team, or leadership position) to achieve better results.

Think of delegation as an investment in your time and energy. By taking the time to identify who is best suited to handle certain tasks, you are investing in the long-term efficiency and productivity of your work. This approach is far more effective than simply cramming your day full of tasks that could be handled by someone else, leaving you with little time to focus on high-priority items.

To overcome the fear of delegation, ask yourself why you're reluctant to let go of tasks. Do you fear subpar results or that it will take too much time to manage? Recognising these thoughts can help shift your mind set from perfectionism to empowerment. Trusting others to handle tasks effectively enables you to focus on the higher-value activities that truly require your attention.

Delegation

## THE DIFFERENT LEVELS OF DELEGATION: UNDERSTANDING THE SCOPE

Delegation is not a one-size-fits-all solution; it's important to understand that there are different levels and scopes of delegation that should align with the complexity of the task and the capabilities of the person to whom you are delegating. Understanding these levels will allow you to delegate with precision and confidence.

1. **Full Delegation:** This is when you pass off a task entirely. The person you delegate to is given full responsibility for the task, from beginning to end. They are expected to complete the task independently, with minimal oversight. Full delegation is appropriate for tasks that are well defined, require little supervision and align well with the capabilities of the individual. This type of delegation is ideal when you need to focus on higher-priority responsibilities that require your attention and expertise.
2. **Partial Delegation:** In this case, you delegate a portion of a task or responsibility but retain some level of involvement or control. For example, you might delegate the research aspect of a project but retain responsibility for presenting the findings. Partial delegation is useful for tasks that are complex or require collaboration, but can be broken down into components that others can handle independently. It's a great middle ground when you want to free up time but still need to stay involved in the overall process.
3. **Supervised Delegation:** This level of delegation involves close guidance and oversight from you while the task is being completed. The person you delegate to is responsible for executing the task but will require feedback and

direction from you at various stages. Supervised delegation is most effective when you are working with someone who is less experienced or new to the task. This allows them to learn while ensuring that the work is done to your standards.

By understanding these levels, you can delegate more strategically and provide the appropriate amount of oversight, which will enhance both your time management and the development of those to whom you are delegating tasks.

*How to Identify Tasks to Delegate*

Effective delegation starts with knowing which tasks to delegate. Not every task on your to-do list is suitable for delegation and part of mastering delegation is learning how to prioritize. There are *two key criteria* to consider when deciding what to delegate:

1. **Tasks that do not require your specific expertise:** These are tasks that, while necessary, do not directly align with your core skills or responsibilities. For instance, administrative work, basic data entry, or routine customer service inquiries may not require your expertise, but they are essential to the smooth functioning of your operation. These tasks are often perfect candidates for delegation, allowing you to free up your time to focus on tasks that align more closely with your strengths and goals.
2. **Tasks that others can do better or more efficiently than you:** This requires a bit of humility and self-awareness. Is there someone on your team (or in your network) who can perform the task with greater speed or skill? By delegating these tasks to someone who is better suited, you ensure

that the work is completed more efficiently and you have more time to focus on areas where you excel.

Once you have identified tasks that meet these criteria, take a moment to assess how delegating them will impact your workload and overall goals. It may also be helpful to consider your longer-term goals. Delegation isn't just about reducing your daily tasks, but about creating the space for more strategic thinking and higher-level decision-making. In this way, delegation becomes a tool not just for better time management, but for improving the quality of your work.

## THE DELEGATION PROCESS: STEPS FOR SUCCESS

It's not enough to simply decide to delegate; you need to have a structured approach to ensure success. Below are some practical steps you can follow to implement delegation effectively:

1. **Assess the task:** What is the nature of the task? How long will it take? What skill sets are required to complete it? Is it a one-off task, or is it something that will need regular attention? The more clearly you define the task, the easier it will be to choose the right person to delegate to.
2. **Choose the right person:** Identify the individual or team best suited to the task. Do they have the necessary skills? Do they have the time and capacity to take it on? Are they interested in the task? When you match the task with the right person, you are more likely to get a better result.
3. **Clearly define the expectations:** Be explicit about what you want to be done. Provide a clear explanation of the task, the desired outcome, and any deadlines. Be transparent about the resources available and what level of support or feedback they can expect from you. The clearer

the instructions, the less room there is for confusion and mistakes.

4. **Provide resources and support:** Make sure the person has everything they need to be successful. This could include training, access to tools, documentation, or specific software. Being prepared to offer support without micromanaging is key to successful delegation, particularly if they are less experienced with the task at hand.

5. **Trust But Verify**: While it's important to trust the person you delegate to, maintaining oversight is equally necessary. Periodically check in on progress, offering guidance if necessary. This balance of autonomy and support ensures the task stays on track.

6. **Foster Open Communication**: Encourage the person you've delegated to reach out if they encounter problems or need clarification. Maintain an open line of communication to address any concerns before they become major issues.

7. **Monitor progress:** Set up a system for checking in and tracking the progress of the task. How often should the person update you? Do they need to check in at specific milestones? Be available for questions and feedback, but avoid micromanaging.

8. **Provide feedback and recognition:** Once the task is completed, provide constructive feedback with actionable advice for next time. Acknowledge the positives and give specific suggestions for areas of improvement. This not only boosts the person's development but also strengthens the delegation process for future tasks.

***Leveraging Delegation for Strategic Success***

Delegation, when done correctly, frees up your time and improves overall productivity. However, it's important to remember that delegation is not about doing less work, it's about focusing on the high-impact tasks that align with your goals and leveraging the strengths of others. By mastering the art of delegation, you not only improve your time management but also empower those around you to contribute in meaningful ways.

**Practical Applications:**

- **Start small**: Begin by delegating minor tasks and gradually increase the responsibility as you gain trust in others' capabilities.
- **Empower others**: When delegating, focus on providing the necessary resources and the confidence to carry out the task independently.
- **Review and refine**: After each delegation, review what worked and what didn't to improve your approach and continue refining your delegation strategy.

Remember, mastering delegation isn't about relinquishing control, it's about strategically choosing what to release so you can focus on what truly matters. By incorporating these principles into your workflow, you'll create a dynamic, collaborative environment where both you and your team can thrive.

## THE BENEFITS OF DELEGATION

When done effectively, delegation brings numerous benefits, not just for your time management but for the growth and success of your team or organisation. By understanding and applying the art of delegation, you unlock efficiencies, foster collaboration, and enhance both individual and collective productivity. Here are some of the most significant advantages:

1. **Increased Efficiency:** One of the most immediate benefits of delegation is increased efficiency. By offloading tasks that others can do, you free up valuable time to focus on higher-priority items, those that require your expertise, strategic insight, or decision-making capabilities. Delegating routine or time-consuming tasks allows you to dedicate more energy and attention to the aspects of your role that drive success. This makes the use of your time more productive and purposeful.
2. **Improved Focus on High-Level Goals:** When you're mired in routine tasks, whether they're administrative duties, logistics, or low-level operations, your focus can easily become fragmented. Delegation enables you to focus on high-level, strategic goals. It allows you to plan, make key decisions and contribute to the long-term vision of your business or organization. With less time spent on low-value tasks, you can drive efforts toward achieving objectives that require your leadership, foresight, and unique expertise.
3. **Skill Development for Others:** Delegation is not just about freeing up your time, it's also an investment in the development of others. By assigning tasks to your colleagues or team members, you give them the opportunity to stretch their abilities, learn new skills, and take on more responsibility. Over time, this empowers them to become more competent and confident in their roles. As people grow in their positions, it benefits the team as a whole by increasing its collective capability. Developing your team's skills can ultimately lead to a

more competent, self-sufficient, and successful workforce.

4. **Stronger Team Collaboration:** When you delegate, you foster a sense of teamwork and collaboration. You show trust in others by recognizing their potential to handle important tasks. This act of entrusting others builds stronger relationships within the team and creates an environment where people feel valued and supported. Team collaboration thrives when there is mutual respect for each other's abilities and a shared sense of purpose. In turn, the culture of cooperation and morale improve, leading to greater success for the organization as a whole.

5. **Prevention of Burnout:** Trying to manage everything on your own can quickly lead to burnout. When you're overwhelmed by the sheer volume of tasks and responsibilities, stress levels rise and productivity declines. Delegation helps prevent burnout by ensuring that the workload is distributed more evenly. It enables you to manage stress better and focus on maintaining a healthy work-life balance. By sharing the load, you ensure that you remain energized, engaged and capable of performing at your best. This approach is essential not only for your well-being but also for the long-term success of your professional efforts.

## LETTING GO TO MOVE FORWARD

Mastering the art of delegation is a transformative step toward better time management and personal growth. It allows you to focus on what matters most, frees up your time and empowers others to contribute toward shared goals. As you learn to delegate effectively, you can shift from being bogged down by tasks to driving results that impact the bigger picture.

Think of delegation as a strategic tool that elevates your efficiency, helps you build a strong team and ensures you maintain balance. It's a way to break free from the trap of micromanagement and the myth of "I can do it all myself." By focusing on the tasks that matter most and trusting others with the rest, you create an environment where everyone has the opportunity to thrive.

Remember, delegation isn't a sign of weakness or failure; on the contrary, it's a smart, efficient practice that enables you to leverage your time and resources effectively. Over time, as you delegate more, you'll find that your time management improves, your focus sharpens and your capacity for achieving your goals increases. The more you practice it, the easier it will become to trust others, freeing up valuable time for you to pursue your highest priorities.

In the end, delegation is about far more than just passing off work, it's about creating a more efficient, collaborative and productive path toward achieving your personal and professional ambitions. By embracing delegation, you not only ease your workload but also build a foundation for sustained success, both for you and your team.

Mastering the art of delegation is one of the most effective ways to improve your time management and unlock your full potential and as you embrace the power of delegation, you will find that your time management improves, your focus sharpens, and your workload becomes more manageable.

# CONCLUSION

As we reach the final pages of this book, I hope you're feeling a renewed sense of clarity, empowerment and confidence. The insights and strategies we've covered were all designed with one central goal: to equip you with practical time management tools that will enhance your productivity and help you create a more balanced and fulfilling work-life dynamic. Whether you're managing a long to-do list, balancing work with personal time, or simply seeking more space for yourself amidst the daily grind, the key message is clear: *effective time management is a skill that anyone can develop*. No matter where you are in your journey, the tools and techniques discussed in this book can help you to unlock more time for what truly matters to empower you to live your life with greater intention.

## REVISITING THE CORE PRINCIPLES

Our journey together began by exploring the psychological barriers to productivity. You learned that the challenges to staying productive aren't always about lack of discipline or motivation.

Psychological factors such as fear of failure, perfectionism, and self-doubt can hold you back, making it difficult to take that first step or remain consistent, particularly with larger projects or new tasks. But here's the empowering truth: by recognising these obstacles, you're already one step ahead. Identifying the psychological traps that hinder your focus enables you to take back control. I hope you've learned that it's okay to face these struggles, they are not unique to you, everyone experiences them and understanding that they're common gives you the strength to work through them.

We also explored how tools like the Pomodoro Technique and task batching can boost focus and efficiency. These strategies provide structure, breaking tasks into smaller, more manageable pieces. By doing so, they make even the most daunting to-do lists feel achievable. Most importantly, you've learned to prioritise your mental and emotional well-being while managing your time. Remember, you are more than a list of tasks; you are a whole person with needs that deserve attention. Creating a fulfilling routine begins with recognising that your mind set shapes how you approach time management.

We dived deep into the importance of setting SMART goals and objectives. It's tempting to set lofty, ambitious objectives, but without clarity, those goals can quickly become overwhelming. I hope that by using the SMART framework; Specific, Measurable, Achievable, Relevant and Time-bound, you now have a clear roadmap for action. This approach isn't just about setting goals; it's about creating a vision that gives you direction and motivation.

Breaking large ambitions into actionable steps helps prevent overwhelm and fosters a sense of accomplishment. Remember, your goals are fluid, life is dynamic and so are your objectives. The flexibility to adjust your goals as circumstances change is critical for maintaining momentum and staying aligned with what truly matters.

Time is one of the most precious resources and learning to use it wisely is essential for success. We learned about the importance of prioritisation. The Eisenhower Matrix helped us sort tasks based on urgency and importance, enabling us to distinguish between what truly needs our attention and what can be delegated or postponed. By embracing task batching, we learned how to focus on similar tasks in blocks of time, minimising distractions and boosting productivity. Prioritisation isn't about doing everything, it's about understanding what aligns most with your long-term goals. Cutting out distractions and investing energy in the right things helps free up time for the activities that bring you closer to your aspirations.

The importance of maintaining physical and psychological well-being for a healthy work-life balance was discussed in detail, as it is such an important part of maintaining an efficient, productive and healthy lifestyle. We discussed in detail the importance of ensuring that your personal life plays a prominent role in life and that you should never just prioritise or focus on work or your career. Having healthy relationships outside of work is also so important. A social life, family life and leisure life all contribute to your overall happiness and productivity in general. A fit mind and body will positively impact your business and career as well as your relationships, so make a conscious effort to have a great work-life balance

We later introduced the concept of delegation. Many of us try to do everything ourselves because of fear that others won't perform tasks to our standards or due to a sense of overwhelming responsibility. However, mastering delegation is a game-changer. By entrusting tasks to others, you not only free up time for yourself but also empower others to contribute and grow. Recognising that no one can do it all alone is crucial. Delegation doesn't mean abandoning responsibility, it's a strategic move to maximise resources and improve efficiency. Start by identifying tasks that can be handled by others, whether at work or at home. Trusting others with responsibilities will lead to better collaboration and reduce stress.

We explored procrastination, an all-too-familiar foe, a thief of time. We examined the psychology behind procrastination, recognizing that it often stems from fear or overwhelm, not laziness. Armed with the knowledge of how to break tasks into smaller, manageable pieces and strategies like the Pomodoro Technique, you have powerful tools to combat procrastination. Remember, procrastination doesn't have to be a vicious cycle of self-criticism. View it as a normal challenge, one that can be overcome with patience and consistency. Every small action you take is a victory. We also focused on mindfulness and the profound impact it can have on time management. By cultivating awareness of the present moment, you reduce stress, enhance focus and improve decision-making throughout the day. Mindfulness doesn't require hours of meditation; it's about staying aware of your thoughts and emotions as you navigate your day. The more present you are, the more intentional you can be with your actions, ensuring that your energy aligns with your highest priorities.

### KEY TAKEAWAYS FOR YOUR NEXT STEPS

Now that we've reflected on the strategies and tools we've covered, let's highlight the most critical lessons that will support your ongoing journey toward effective time management:

1. **Recognise and Overcome Obstacles**: Productivity barriers like procrastination, perfectionism, and fear of failure are common to everyone. By identifying your psychological obstacles, you've already gained the power to navigate them. Remember, it's not about eliminating obstacles, it's about learning how to manage them. Tools like the Pomodoro Technique, task batching, and the Eisenhower Matrix can help you stay focused and productive, even when distractions arise.
2. **Set SMART Goals**: Clear, actionable goals provide purpose and direction. By setting SMART goals; Specific, Measurable, Achievable, Relevant, and Time-bound, you ensure that your goals are attainable and aligned with your broader vision. Be flexible with your goals, they should evolve as your circumstances do. Reviewing and refining your goals keeps you aligned with your purpose.
3. **Prioritise What Matters**: Knowing the difference between urgent and important tasks is essential. Using prioritisation tools like the Eisenhower Matrix ensures your time is spent on activities that contribute to your long-term goals, rather than getting lost in the noise of less critical tasks. Task batching helps streamline your workload, allowing you to focus on what truly matters.
4. **Tackle Procrastination**: Procrastination is a common struggle, but it's manageable. Break tasks into smaller, more approachable pieces and use time-blocking techniques like the Pomodoro Technique to stay on track. Be kind to yourself when you slip up, every small step forward counts. Celebrate every victory, no matter how minor.
5. **Embrace Mindfulness**: Stay present, intentional and aware in your daily actions. Mindfulness reduces stress and improves your focus, decision-making and time

management. By checking in with yourself and adjusting as needed, you can better manage your energy and stay aligned with your goals.

6. **Delegate**: Don't hesitate to let go of tasks that don't require your direct involvement. Delegation frees up valuable time and can lead to greater collaboration. Trust others with responsibilities, they'll contribute to the success of the team and you'll find that letting go of some tasks can improve overall efficiency.
7. **Celebrate Your Successes**: Time management isn't just about productivity; it's also about enjoying the process. Celebrate your wins, no matter how small. Acknowledge the progress you've made and give yourself credit for the hard work you've put in. Recognising your achievements boosts motivation and keeps you moving forward.
8. **Take Care of Yourself**: Self-care is a crucial component of any successful time management strategy. Prioritising your well-being, mentally, physically and emotionally, ensures you have the energy to dedicate to your tasks. Make time for relaxation, exercise, hobbies and quality time with loved ones. Proper balance comes from caring for yourself first so that you can show up fully for everything else.

Achieving work-life balance isn't about finding the perfect formula or achieving a fixed state of equilibrium. It's about consistently evaluating your priorities, setting healthy boundaries and remaining adaptable as circumstances shift.

By practicing mindfulness, prioritizing self-care and integrating both your work and personal responsibilities in a way that works for you, you can create a life that feels meaningful, fulfilling and in harmony with your goals.

It's not about achieving perfection; it's about creating a sustainable and flexible lifestyle that reflects your core values and enables you to thrive both personally and professionally.

So now that you've reflected on these strategies, it's time to take action. Start by integrating the techniques that resonated most with you into your daily routine. Choose one or two to focus on initially and experiment with them. As you become more comfortable, gradually incorporate more strategies. There's no one-size-fits-all approach, what works for one person may not work for another. The key is to find what works best for you and stick with it.

Time management is a skill that requires practice and patience. The more you implement these tools, the more natural they'll become, the more ingrained into your day to day routines. It's time to put the strategies into practice and start seeing the positive changes in your productivity, balance and overall life satisfaction.

**If you enjoyed this book and found it helpful, we would appreciate it if you left a favourable review on Amazon.**

# GLOSSARY OF TERMS

**80/20 Rule (Pareto Principle)**
A principle suggesting that 80% of outcomes come from 20% of efforts. Identifying and focusing on the highest-impact tasks can maximize productivity with minimal effort.

**ABCDE Method**
A prioritization technique that assigns tasks a letter from A to E based on urgency and importance, where "A" tasks are the highest priority and "E" tasks are the lowest. The method provides a structured approach to managing time effectively.

**Batch Processing**
A productivity technique involving the grouping of similar tasks to complete them in one session. This reduces time lost in task-switching and increases focus on repetitive tasks.

**Biological Prime Time**
The time of day when an individual's energy and mental sharpness are at their peak. Recognising one's prime time allows for scheduling high-priority tasks during these periods.

**Boundaries**
Limits set to protect personal time and prevent work from encroaching on personal life. Boundaries are essential for maintaining work-life balance and reducing burnout.

**Burnout**
A state of emotional, mental and often physical exhaustion caused by prolonged stress and overwork. Effective time management practices can help prevent burnout.

**Calendar Blocking**
A method of organizing tasks by scheduling dedicated time slots on a calendar. This helps visualise workload and maintain control over time commitments.

**Delegate**
The act of assigning tasks to others to manage workload more effectively. Delegation is a key skill in maximising productivity and focusing on high-priority activities.

**Deep Work**
Intense, focused work completed without distractions, often leading to high-quality output. Allocating time for deep work can improve efficiency and support complex tasks.

**Digital Detox**
A break from digital devices to reduce distractions and improve focus. Taking periodic digital detoxes can enhance productivity and mental clarity.

**Distractions**
External or internal interruptions that divert attention away from tasks. Minimising distractions is crucial for maintaining focus and productivity.

**Eisenhower Matrix**
A prioritisation tool that divides tasks into four quadrants based on urgency and importance: 1) Urgent and Important, 2) Important but Not Urgent, 3) Urgent but Not Important and 4) Not Urgent and Not Important. This method helps professionals focus on what truly matters.

**Energy Management**
A strategy that focuses on maximising energy levels for better productivity rather than simply managing time. Managing energy allows professionals to work efficiently without overextending.

**Focus Time**
A period dedicated to uninterrupted work on a specific task. Focus time helps achieve a state of flow and complete tasks more efficiently.

**Goal Setting**
The process of defining and planning desired outcomes. Clear goal setting helps align time management strategies with long-term objectives.

**Intentional Living**
A lifestyle approach where actions align with personal values and goals. Intentional living supports a balanced life and prioritises meaningful work.

**Mindfulness**
The practice of being fully present and engaged in the moment. Mindfulness can improve focus, reduce stress and support better time management.

**Multitasking**
Attempting to perform multiple tasks simultaneously. Studies show that multitasking can reduce productivity and increase errors, making single-tasking a more effective strategy.

**Over commitment**
Agreeing to more tasks than time allows, leading to stress and diminished productivity. Learning to manage commitments is essential for effective time management.

## GLOSSARY OF TERMS | 107

**Parkinson's Law**
The adage that work expands to fill the time available for its completion. Setting strict deadlines can counteract Parkinson's Law and increase efficiency.

**Pomodoro Technique**
A time management method where work is broken into 25-minute intervals, or "Pomodoros," separated by short breaks. This technique improves focus, reduces fatigue and enhances productivity over long periods.

**Prioritisation**
The process of ranking tasks by their importance and urgency. Effective prioritisation helps professionals focus on high-impact activities that align with their goals.

**Procrastination**
The act of delaying tasks despite potential consequences. Understanding and overcoming procrastination is crucial for effective time management.

**Productivity**
The measure of output relative to input, typically in terms of time. Improving productivity allows professionals to accomplish more within a set time frame.

**Reflection Time**
A period set aside to review goals, evaluate progress, and make adjustments. Regular reflection promotes self-awareness and helps refine time management strategies.

**SMART Goals**
A goal-setting framework where goals are Specific, Measurable, Achievable, Relevant and Time-bound. SMART goals provide clarity, focus and structure to enhance goal attainment.

**Stress Management**
Techniques used to control and reduce stress. Effective time management reduces stress by preventing last-minute work and overwhelming workloads.

**Task Batching**
The grouping of similar tasks to complete them in one session. Task batching minimises time lost to switching between tasks, thereby improving productivity.

**Time Audit**
An analysis of how time is spent over a given period, helping individuals identify time-wasting activities and make adjustments to improve efficiency.

**Time Blocking**
A time management technique where specific blocks of time are dedicated to individual tasks. Time blocking creates structure and minimises decision fatigue.

**Time Tracking**

The act of recording and reviewing how time is spent on tasks. Time tracking provides insights into productivity and helps identify areas for improvement.

**To-Do List**

A list of tasks that need to be completed, often organised by priority. A well-organised to-do list aids in task management and ensures that nothing is overlooked.

**Zero-Based Scheduling**

A scheduling approach where each hour is intentionally planned, allowing for no unallocated time. Zero-based scheduling maximizes productivity by reducing idle time.

**Work-Life Balance**

The state of equilibrium where professional responsibilities do not overwhelm personal life. Effective time management promotes a healthy balance, leading to greater satisfaction and well-being.

# REFERENCES

Dweck, C. S. (2006). *Mind set: The new psychology of success*. Random House. https://www.penguinrandomhouse.com/books/44330/mindset-by-carol-s-dweck-phd/

Champion Health. (n.d.). *10 mind blowing benefits of mindfulness at work*. Champion Health. https://www.championhealth.co.uk/

FasterCapital. (n.d.). *Time management strategies: Continuous improvement – The time management journey – Embracing continuous improvement*. FasterCapital. https://fastercapital.com/content/Time-Management-Strategies--Continuous-Improvement---The-Time-Management-Journey--Embracing-Continuous-Improvement.html

Forbes. (2023, August 6). *The productivity problem with remote work*. Forbes. https://www.forbes.com/sites/tracybrower/2023/08/06/the-productivity-problem-with-remote-work/

Hubstaff. (n.d.). *Top 10 time management challenges*. Hubstaff Blog. https://hubstaff.com/blog/time-management-challenges/

IE University. (n.d.). *Procrastination psychology: Understanding effects, causes, and strategies*. IE University. https://www.ie.edu/center-for-health-and-well-being/blog/procrastination-psychology-effects-causes-strategies/

Kumanu. (n.d.). *Defining work-life balance: Its history and future*. Kumanu. https://www.kumanu.com/defining-work-life-balance-its-history-and-future/

Mind Tools Content Team. (n.d.). *Kaizen: A strategy for continuous improvement*. Mind Tools. https://www.mindtools.com

Imai, M. (1986). *Kaizen: The key to Japan's competitive success*. McGraw-Hill. https://www.scirp.org/reference/referencespapers?referenceid=2019198

Schoolbox. (n.d.). *The impact of self-assessment & self-reflection on learning*. Schoolbox. https://schoolbox.education/blog/what-does-self-assessment-and-self-reflection-bring-to-the-learning-journey/

Suziswartz.com. (n.d.). *How the Pomodoro technique saved my productivity and helped me as a writer*. Suzi Swartz. https://www.suziswartz.com/how-the-pomodoro-technique-saved-my-productivity-and-helped-me-as-a-writer/

Teekay Rezeaumerah. (2023, Jan 23). *Digital minimalism: Where to start, what to aim for, no BS!*. Medium. https://teekayrezeaumerah.medium.com/digital-minimalism-where-to-start-what-to-aim-for-no-bs-b62caea7ce03

Upbase. (2024, Oct 21). *The ABCDE method explained: How to use it effectively*. Upbase Blog. https://upbase.io/blog/how-to-use-the-abcde-method-effectively/

Verywell Mind. (2020, April 05). *Top 10 stress-relieving hobbies*. Verywell Mind. https://www.verywellmind.com/top-stress-reliever-hobbies-3144592

Wellspring Prevention. (2023, Jul 26). *9 self-care tips for busy professionals*. Wellspring Prevention. https://wellspringprevention.org/blog/self-care-busy-professionals/

Psychology Today. (2024, June 26). *From small steps to big wins: The importance of celebrating*. Psychology Today. https://www.psychologytoday.com/us/blog/empower-your-mind/202406/from-small-steps-to-big-wins-the-importance-of-celebrating

Eisenhower. (n.d.). *The Eisenhower matrix: Introduction & 3-minute video tutorial*. Eisenhower.me. https://www.eisenhower.me/eisenhower-matrix/

Hubstaff. (n.d.). *How to do a time audit (with actionable steps)*. Hubstaff. https://hubstaff.com/time-tracking/time-audit

Atlassian. (2023, Dec 26). *How to write SMART goals*. https://www.atlassian.com/blog/productivity/how-to-write-smart-goals

ProductPlan. (n.d.). *PDCA cycle*. https://www.productplan.com/glossary/pdca-cycle/

EdPsyched. (2023, March 20). *The Pomodoro technique: Overcome procrastination*. https://www.edpsyched.co.uk/blog/pomodoro-technique-overcome-procrastination

National Institute of General Medical Sciences. (2023, Sept). *Circadian rhythms*. https://www.nigms.nih.gov/education/fact-sheets/Pages/circadian-rhythms.aspx

Study.com. (2023, Nov). *What is Kaizen in management? Definition, examples & process*. https://study.com/academy/lesson/what-is-kaizen-in-management-definition-examples-process.html

# ABOUT THE PUBLISHER

**Freedom Publications** is a respected name in business literature, dedicated to providing readers from all walks of life with the tools and insights to succeed in today's competitive and ever-evolving world. Our books cater to teams, leaders, managers, entrepreneurs, professionals, executives and everyday individuals eager to sharpen their skills, elevate their thinking and make impactful changes in their careers and lives.

Each publication by Freedom Publications is carefully crafted to deliver practical, accessible guidance on everything from building cohesive teams and inspiring effective leadership to boosting productivity and achieving personal and professional goals. With a focus on real-world applications, our books empower readers to turn concepts into actionable strategies that benefit both individuals and groups, enabling stronger communication, smarter decision-making and sustained success across any field.

Whether you are a business leader striving to lead your team with vision, a professional looking to grow your skill set, an entrepreneur ready to take your venture to the next level, or simply someone interested in improving everyday effectiveness, Freedom Publications is your essential resource for the insights and knowledge to thrive in every aspect of modern business.

**If you enjoyed this book and found it helpful, we would appreciate it if you left a favourable review on Amazon.**

www.ingramcontent.com/pod-product-compliance
Lightning Source LLC
Chambersburg PA
CBHW050439010526
44118CB00013B/1602